To Katie -

May God
bless you richly -
Thanks for the
great job you do!

Anne Doray Koomans
7-7-21

by
Anne Davey
Koomans

Beyond Barriers

Second Edition

ReadersMagnet, LLC

by
Anne Davey
Koomans

Beyond Barriers

Second Edition

ReadersMagnet, LLC

Dedication

THIS BOOK IS dedicated to Dave's mom, Helen Simpson; his brother, Max; and his sisters, Marilyn Zidel, and Janet Hatfield. Because of their love, enthusiasm, sense of humor, and concern for Dave, he grew up feeling loved, and knew it was his destiny to use their examples to help others.

Acknowledgement

A VERY SPECIAL ACKNOWLEDGEMENT to Roberta Gotham, with much gratitude for the many hours she spent reading, editing, advising and discussing the contents of this book with me.

Thanks also to Bob Weir and Encore magazine for a great story they published about Dave, which motivated us to write this book. Bob suggested the title.

Introduction

$\mathscr{H}$AVE YOU EVER slept in a lovely hotel room full of Black Widow Spiders? Have you ever held a ship in port for several hours as the staff devised a plan to get you aboard so they could depart? Have you ever slept on the floor in the President's Suite of the famous Grand Hotel on Mackinac Island? Have you been a guest in the Penthouse of the New York Hilton, sleeping in the same room where President Kennedy slept? Dave and I have.

David Davey recognized his purpose in life when he was still in college, and spent the rest of his life fulfilling that purpose. In so doing, he made a difference in the lives of most people.

Dave started addressing the many areas of barriers in this country that needed to be changed. He was concerned for anyone whose life circumstances are a barrier to work and a normal life. He wanted this book to be written to inspire people who meet a person in a wheelchair to see past the chair. Using a wheelchair does not define who you are. One's attitude will help determine if he or she is going to enjoy life or have a lifelong pity party. Dave looked for the good in life and people, and found it.

When we were laying out the book, Dave asked me to include his chapter on "Yes Men in Wheelchairs Have Sex." He hoped to help educate the public that men and women in wheelchairs have the same desires and hopes as you, the reader. After you have read the chapter, I hope that you are glad we included it.

A few stories from business trips and vacations are included. A good sense of humor helped us to laugh at the situation when we needed to transform barrier free rooms into "truly accessible rooms." Close your eyes and try to picture some of the situations in the book. You'll feel like you personally knew David M. Davey.

Contents

Chapter 1

A Life Changed By Polio

DAVE NEVER FORGOT that life-changing morning. He and his family were spending a weekend on his Uncle Murvil's farm. He and his brother, Max, played football in the barnyard on Friday night with relatives. His parents, Max and Helen Davey, and his younger sisters, Marilyn and Janet, were among the spectators. When he awoke Saturday morning, David thought he had the flu. His head ached, his eyes were blurry, and his mouth tasted like the fish he ate Friday night. When he jumped out of bed, and found himself on the floor, he couldn't understand why his twelve-year-old legs, that had been so strong when he played football the night before, wouldn't hold him up. As soon as she saw Dave, his mom was sure that he had polio.

It was during the terrible polio epidemic of the 1940's. Most public swimming areas and amusement parks closed for two or three summers to prevent spreading this feared disease. At that time, it was known by the dreaded name of Infantile Paralysis.

Dave's parents took him to the doctor immediately. He was just one of many people who entered the hospital to either get well or leave in the metal box. He spent over five months in an iron lung, and another four months going through rehabilitation therapy.

David Davey, in Iron Lung with his Dad.

David Davey in iron lung when he had polio, talking to his dad, Maxfield Davey

The iron lung looked like a large frozen juice can with a mechanism that made a vacuum, creating the pressure Dave needed for breathing. His head stuck through a hole in the other end, with a spongy collar creating a tight seal around his neck. As the membrane compressed, it forced air in and out of his mouth and nose, a function similar to the bi-pap machine Dave used for sleeping in the 21ˢᵗ century. There was a mirror above him so he could see what was happening behind him.

The treatments were very painful. The nurses and aides soaked heavy coarse wool blankets in steaming hot water. Using a manual wringer like those on wringer washing machines, they wrung out the excess water, and wrapped the steaming blankets around Dave's legs. What pain he endured. Although he couldn't see what they were doing, I'm sure the boiling hot blankets caused blisters, and it was hard for a 12-year-old boy not to cry. Most did. Even though he couldn't move his legs, he still had feeling throughout his body. He tried to be brave. He must have been convincing, because his mom never realized he was frightened. Every time she came, she'd compliment Dave on being her "brave young man". It wasn't easy living up to that title.

Dave was very frightened as he lay in the iron lung and heard the "death wagon" coming down the hallway to remove one more patient who wouldn't be leaving alive. This usually happened at night, with very little lighting in the hallway. The coffin-like box, sitting on top of the wagon, had a sound of metal flapping against metal, and wheels that had their own eerie squeak. As it came down the dimly-lit hallway toward their room, some children screamed or cried, some sucked their blanket as they tried to muffle their whimpering; and some, like Dave, lay speechless, but frozen with fear. Each boy feared that was his coffin approaching. Months later, as surviving patients emerged from iron lungs, many of them lay on their beds, hiding under their blankets as the 'death wagon' approached, while others lay sobbing.

The nurses and doctors talked about death, and those they thought wouldn't make it, as though the children weren't there. Sometimes Dave knew they were talking about him, but his mother would smile and let everyone know that God had a plan for Dave. At night, Dave often shook with fear, and sometimes wondered if people pushing the 'death wagon' were, indeed, coming for him.

Many patients came into the hospital and died after several days, having had no visitors. Most people were afraid they would catch the polio, or take it home to their other kids.

Dave's family members visited him every opportunity they had. The hospital food was so terrible that, at least once a day, Dave's mom brought him fried chicken and mashed potatoes, beef and noodles, spaghetti, hamburgers, French fries, milkshakes, or other food she knew he liked. How he looked forward to those meals. Dave was convinced he would have died of starvation if she hadn't. I'm sure some children did. Many were skin and bones when they were put into the 'death wagon'.

Dave was a normal size kid weighing about 100 pounds when he entered the hospital. When he heard others crying because they were hungry, or because they felt everyone had abandoned them, Dave thanked God for his family. Even with the nourishing food Dave's mom brought him once or twice daily, Dave was down to 50 pounds when his brother Max carried him out of the hospital nine months later.

Dave was 11 when he accepted Christ as his personal Savior. During the nine months he was in the hospital, Dave had a chance to review every wrong thing he had ever done. He felt certain there had to be a reason why God was punishing him.

Dave confessed to God and his mom every sin he remembered. He apologized for every lie he had told and every time he had been rude to Mom, Dad, Max, and about everyone else he knew. He began to see Jesus as his friend as well as his Savior. It was a spiritual growth experience. Dave's mom had an opportunity to tell him about the grace that God gives, assuring and reassuring him that he got this disease because there was an epidemic, not because God was punishing him. His mom was good at knowing what he was thinking.

Long-forgotten memories filled his mind as he had hour after hour to review them. Before polio, he and his family rode the train to his Uncle Walter's farm, near Frankfort, Indiana, during their summer school break. When they were young, Dave and his brother Max enjoyed themselves profoundly on the train. They had discovered that any time they flushed the toilet, everything in it emptied between the tracks. Their fun ended abruptly one year when Mom caught on to their shenanigans.

Dave figured that God wasn't pleased when he and Max had contests regarding their aim as they wet on Uncle Walter's hogs. Max usually won. Times when they were supposed to stay in the farmyard, but decided to go exploring, swirled in Dave's mind. During their secret adventures, they were often gone for hours. The memory of his family's relief when he and Max returned safely brought back feelings of guilt.

In the iron lung, Dave recalled the thrill of leaving Detroit for the summer, and accompanying Uncle Walter as they slopped the hogs, and rode on the tractor that had no rubber tires. Since rubber was used for World War II equipment for the American troops in the 1940's, it was unavailable for tractor tires. Dave had to smile as his mind pictured that tractor.

Dave remembered falling asleep in the upstairs bedroom of the white centennial farmhouse, as his nose picked up the farm smells, his ears the sounds, and his eyes the stars of the night filling the unpolluted sky. The sound of the farm, late at night, as birds and animals seemed to close another day, was such a good memory. As the sun went down, the chatter of birds was noisy, then lower and lower until Dave imagined they were whispering goodnight to their families.

Memories flashed through Dave's mind in the hospital, hour after hour, until he could almost smell the sweat on Uncle Walter's cows, hogs, and horses. It helped him forget the smells of the hospital and death.

How Dave loved hearing the distant forlorn sound of the train's whistle in the night as it passed the railroad crossing a few miles from the Indiana farm. He could never understand why the whistle of trains near the hospital sounded so harsh.

Thoughts of his Aunt Ella, Uncle Walter, and cousin, Anna, brought a myriad of wonderful memories, and reminded Dave of how kind they were to him and his family. They always made him feel loved.

During the hours in the iron lung, Dave's mind pictured the dangerous steps to their Indiana cellar. The steps had been there since the house was built. Every day Aunt Ella and Anna gathered eggs from the hen house. They carried them down those crumbling cement steps to the cool cellar, then cleaned and graded the eggs for grocery stores. The crated eggs remained in the cellar until a grocery truck driver picked them up twice a week. The driver felt the steps were too dangerous, so Aunt Ella carried the crates up to him. Dave never understood the man letting her do this. Going up and down the steps seemed even more dangerous for Aunt Ella because she always wore the black shoes with laces and fat high heels, that were popular for housewives in the 1930's and 40's.

When Dave asked other kids in the hospital ward what they had done wrong before coming down with polio, they couldn't think of anything. That convinced Dave that he had to be the worst kid in the world. At the time, in the hospital, his young life looked pretty bad to him. He realized he had been anything but perfect.

As he lay on his back, in the iron lung, Dave dreamt of the days in his Grandpa and Grandma Heaton's barn, where he and Max swung, barefoot, down on the ropes to the cement floor. He could picture that floor, loaded with nails, broken glass, and so many other things. Their feet could have been cut severely if the brothers hadn't landed on the little square in the middle that was free of most debris.

Memories of his Grandpa and Grandma Heaton swirled in his head. Even though Dave was young when his grandpa died, he remembered the rules and truths his grandpa taught him, and his grandpa's generosity with the family when they didn't have much money. His grandpa bought and sold meat for a living. He provided Dave's family with all of their meat. Dave smiled as he recalled times when his Grandpa Heaton went to the store to get ice cream cones for the family. As he came around the side of the house to the children's window, his grandpa handed ice cream cones to them, and pretended no one else in the family was aware. Dave and his peers were convinced they had a great secret with their grandpa. It was important to his grandpa that each of his grandchildren knew the Lord, and strived to be a young person of integrity. As Dave lay there remembering his wonderful grandpa, he was convinced he had failed him miserably.

His grandma had always bought most of the family's clothes. A frown crossed his face when he remembered some of those clothes. Many other boys in the 1940's were stuck with wearing knickers to school, but not one boy was happy for the opportunity.

Thoughts of his immediate past made Dave realize what a pain in the side he must have been to Max, his 14-year-old brother. Sometimes when he lay awake at night, he wondered if Max would be better off if he died. That possibility made him cry. Before polio, Dave always followed Max, and insisted on being a part of his crowd. Of course Max and his friends loved to tackle Dave when they played football. Dave loved running with the ball, and thought they let him participate because they liked him. Now he doubted if they did.

Since he wasn't any good at baseball, the kids at school made Dave the umpire. Max had to save Dave more than once when the kids threatened his demise on the way home from school because of his poor judgment calls. As he lay there, he was convinced that the kids probably would have killed him if Max had not been willing to intervene. Tears filled Dave's eyes as he lay there, loving Max for his compassion.

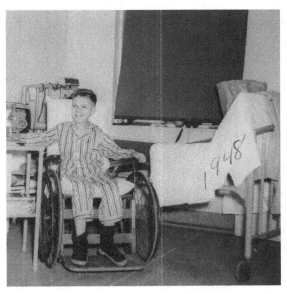

David Davey on February 13, 1948, after he had
lost 50 pounds because of the polio

After five months in the iron lung, Dave moved to the Physical Therapy Unit. After months of physical therapy, it was evident that Dave's leg muscles would not hold him up. Although he couldn't use crutches, his arms and muscles were strong enough that he could use a wheelchair.

When Dave left the hospital in 1949, the doctors sent him home, knowing there was nothing more they could do. They told his parents not to waste any money sending him to college because he would not live past his middle twenties. His mom told them she knew God had a plan for Dave's life. Of course her comments were good for Dave's morale because his family probably believed his mom and God were partners. I know Dave did.

The doctors warned his parents that it was imperative that Dave should not be out in the cold for the next twelve months because his lungs would collapse. When Dave's parents heard that a very bad winter was expected for 1949–50, they sold their house; his dad quit his job; and the family moved to Florida. Dave's Grandma Heaton bought the family a new station wagon with wood trim. Dave laughed when he remembered that he and his peers felt like they were millionaires, having a spiffy vehicle like that. Knowing they were headed to far-away Florida gave credibility to their thoughts. As a child, Dave never realized what sacrifices family and friends were making to keep him alive. He just knew how special he felt.

Dave loved the heat and sandy beaches when they arrived in Florida. He often lay on the beach while his family covered him with the warm sand until only his head was showing. It helped his body soak up the heat. When his dad couldn't get a job, his parents canned jellies and jam to sell. Dave's Grandma Heaton sent some money as well. Although his parents did everything they could, the family was forced to move back to Detroit in the spring.

Since the warmth in Florida was so therapeutic for him, Dave was sorry they were leaving Florida. Dave later told the kids and me that he realized God had to get him back to Michigan so he could graduate from Wayne State University, get into Goodwill, and eventually meet me. He was so grateful God had the whole picture. Me too!

Dave missed going to school with friends he had in his life before polio. The school system was unprepared to serve the many polio survivors who used crutches or wheelchairs.

The Detroit Board of Education started a homebound learning program. Teachers brought homework to a student's house twice a week. The work was supposed to keep students busy for two or three days, but Dave finished the assignments in less than an hour, while the teacher was still talking to his mom.

Next, Dave attended a special school for handicapped children. Most of the kids didn't know any of the other students. Dave couldn't remember any of the kids bonding or becoming friends with other survivors. From their comments, Dave could tell that many of the kids didn't expect to live very long; some didn't. It never occurred to Dave that he might not.

Max was kind enough to carry Dave on his back into his friends' houses that weren't wheelchair accessible, and where they watched TV shows their mom had forbidden them to see. He led a pretty normal life for a teenager because of Max's generosity and his sister Marilyn's willingness to push him into areas where he could not take his own wheelchair. There was nothing they did or saw on TV that would be forbidden in today's world for a five-year-old. How times have changed.

All of his neighborhood friends asked Dave when he was going to attend school with them. Dave bugged his mom, and she bugged Mr. Emmons, the principal of Cooley High School where Max attended. Mr. Emmons lived in Dave's neighborhood, so Dave's mom waited many afternoons until she saw Mr. Emmons walking home from school, and would question him about when Dave could switch schools. With Mom's relentless pursuit, Mr. Emmons finally obtained special permission from the Detroit Board of Education to allow Dave to go to Cooley High School with his friends for his junior and senior years.

Grandma Heaton bought Dave his first car, a shiny new black 1953 Ford. It made him feel "normal" not to have to always rely on others for transportation. The car also made his mom's life a lot easier.

Dave was so grateful to be there with his friends. Many times he told the children and me that he wished he could thank the janitor who memorized his class schedule, and took him up or down on the service elevator. Sometimes he rode next to garbage cans, and sometimes he believed he could taste the dust from the blackboard erasers. He became a member of the Honor Society, and his classmates elected Dave President of his senior class.

After the school officials evaluated Dave's attendance, and deemed it successful, they changed their policy the year after Dave graduated, and allowed wheelchair users to attend Detroit Public Schools.

Dave and Max went with their friends to church youth meetings and singspirations, wherever the girls were. In the 1950's, church was where most people met someone to date. Max and his friends let Dave tag along in their cars when they drove around the drive-in restaurants. When there was an opening next to a carload of girls, they parked there. The boys tried talking the girls into coming to their youth meetings or they'd find out what church the girls attended and visit there.

In high school, Dave's love for photography and film developing increased. He enjoyed dabbling in his darkroom at home, and his first job was developing pictures at a local shop during high school and college.

Life had to be hard getting Dave into the house when there was snow on the ground and the ramp. All of his family had to make sacrifices to assure his success in life. He couldn't remember any of them ever grumbling.

Although many people thought Dave's health was back to normal, the muscles of his body always felt weak. His parents pursued every miracle cure that was advertised. Dave had physical therapy, and went to religious healers and many quacks. All the religious healers and quacks tried to make him feel guilty. They told Dave and his family they knew he could walk if he wanted to.

Finally, a doctor in Ohio with a small office in his home, known for his work with post-polio patients, took swatches from Dave's nose, saliva, and throat. As Dave's family looked through the microscope, it was scary to see that Dave still had active polio cells in his body. The doctor warned him that his throat and nose would be sore after he took several swatches. The doctor also needed as much saliva as Dave could give him. The doctor used the swatches and saliva to prepare a liquid antidote. He said the antidote should prevent Dave from having future repercussions from the polio. It took awhile for the doctor to prepare it.

When the antidote was ready, Dave's family returned to Ohio. The doctor explained Dave's lungs and muscles were at their maximum development. Motor muscles were gone from his legs; and he would be at his maximum strength when the antidote took hold. He warned Dave against using crutches and draining his energy by dragging his feet. He was kind, and refused to accept any money.

Within a few weeks, Dave's strength returned, and he felt stronger than he had since he had the polio; he was no longer exhausted all the time. When Dave's family returned in a month for a follow-up, new swatches showed Dave was polio-free. The doctor told Dave's parents not to waste any more money on quacks. Other than being unable to walk, the doctor said Dave should be able to lead a pretty normal life after that with a fairly normal life expectancy. The doctor encouraged Dave to learn what his energy capacity was, and to listen to his body if it told him to slow down. Dave didn't remember the doctor's name.

Chapter 2

Finding Purpose in His Life

AVE APPRECIATED GETTING to attend Wayne State University (WSU), although some of his classes took a lot of energy going from one classroom to the next. During most of his five years at WSU, he held three jobs. The position he enjoyed most was Lighting and Control Panel Technician for plays and other events. He was also a Dorm Counselor at WSU, and continued to develop films at a local business as a third job.

Unfortunately, it was an accepted belief that occupants of wheelchairs, with a college education, would want to make a living as an accountant. By Dave's third year at WSU he felt trapped. Fortunately, his Accounting professor saw that Dave had no interest in his class, and agreed to give him a passing grade only if Dave would switch his major to Business Administration.

Dave's roommate, Dick Wooten, a preacher's kid, was a little worldlier than Dave, as well as a head taller and probably seventy pounds heavier. Although Dick was a polio survivor and used a wheelchair, he was strong. Dick was an older teenager, with fully developed shoulders, chest, and lungs when he was stricken with the disease. Dick had a great sense of humor. He and Dave laughed a lot, and Dick taught Dave not to take himself too seriously. Other students dropped by their room to watch their evening contest of popping wheelies. Dave said it was a hoot trying to keep up with Dick.

RECOGNIZING HIS PURPOSE IN LIFE

When Dave and Dick sat around in their room, they often discussed services and equipment they would like to see available to wheelchair users. They had big dreams of how they could personally make a difference in "their" world. Ironically, neither of them saw himself as handicapped. They were both grateful that they had gotten scholarships to Wayne State University, but, looking into the future, knew there would be thousands of people in wheelchairs because of polio, wars, or accidents, who wouldn't be so blessed. They were concerned about what future would be available for those individuals if they couldn't afford a college education. They believed God had spared them and put them together at WSU for a reason. The reason, they felt, was to encourage each other to fulfill God's purpose in their lives. They were confident that God would give them the ability to help people receive the training, knowledge, and equipment to allow them to succeed.

Dick felt he should explore ways to provide affordable private vehicles to the men and women who couldn't use public transportation. It was obvious to him that a person couldn't hold a job unless he or she was able to arrive at their employment on time. Dave and Dick had cars with hand controls and other needed equipment. They had a friend who was a quadriplegic. He couldn't ride in either of their cars because he was unable to make the transfer from his chair to the car. Since his wheelchair wasn't collapsible, it wouldn't fit in their cars or up the steps of city buses. Dick felt most quadriplegics could drive if their chair would fit into a properly equipped vehicle.

Dick knew it was his destiny to communicate with manufacturers. They needed to know the need for invention and production of the equipment necessary for America's wheelchair users, and people with other handicaps, to succeed. He and Dave envisioned buses and private vans with affordable chair lifts. The need, as he saw it, seemed to drive Dick to get his degree so he could get started.

Dave believed his destiny was to help people have the opportunity to make a decent living. He knew this was only possible if they could obtain jobs they were capable of doing. He felt God would help him to educate the public that people with disabilities should have that opportunity. He was convinced God wanted him to make a difference by developing rehabilitation programs for people who needed that service. Dave also knew people had to have some practical experience to get a job. His desire to not be an accountant gave him compassion to prevent others from being ensnared by a similar fate. Physical Therapy was still developing in the 1960's, and today's Occupational Therapy was still a dream away. Selling pencils and making baskets, much of the 1950/60's therapy, didn't appeal to either of the men.

HOMELESS IN THE 1960's

There was a man who temporarily lived in a hole in the ground on, or next to, the campus at Wayne State University. Dave didn't know how long he lived there, but didn't think it was very long. When he and Dick Wooten heard about it, they had to check it out. Dave said it looked like the huge slab of cement, serving as the man's roof, had been a driveway or sidewalk at one time. A fear that the ground might cave in with their wheelchairs, kept them from getting close enough to see down in the hole. Dave and Dick wondered if someday they could do something so people like the man could work and live in decent housing.

Some students couldn't understand how the man kept from getting wet down there, but others told Dave it looked perfectly dry.

He was told the man had old coats and ragged blankets wrapped all around him. Dave remembered the man smiled and spoke kindly to him the one time he saw him. The next time Dave went by, the hole was filled in. The man's situation made quite an impression on students who wondered why he was there. Dave suggested WSU let him live there as a motivation for students to get their degrees, and not have to share that hole. Shortly before Dave died, we read an article in the *Kalamazoo Gazette* of homeless persons in Kalamazoo. Dave said he has often wondered what happened to the man in the hole.

Chapter 3

Goodwill—A Life-Changing Experience

ORTUNATELY FOR DAVE, Dick Wooten took a job at the Detroit Goodwill when he finished college. Dick called and told Dave to come to Goodwill and take the executive training. He told Dave about the training and said he loved it, and thought the opportunities at Goodwill would allow both of them to fulfill their destinies. Before he went for the interview, Dave never thought he'd consider it, but once he learned what Goodwill was all about, it sounded great. On July 1, 1960, Detroit Goodwill hired him for their Sales Director position. Their Board was trying to decide whether to keep their stores open or to close them. Goodwill Industries of America (GIA) had Dave take the executive training course at the same time.

It was a good thing because sales in all the Detroit retail stores continued in their three-year slump. Dave received a wonderful evaluation from GIA after he completed the executive training in 1961. However, his annual review by the Detroit Goodwill was so bad they fired him from the staff position. Goodwill Industries of America (GIA) immediately sent Dave to Sandusky, Ohio to start a small branch for the Toledo Goodwill. They wanted to see if he'd sink or swim.

SANDUSKY, OHIO

Dave immediately hired a good Retail Store Sales Manager, and soon Sandusky's retail store was doing well. After a short time, Dave personally visited local companies, and he soon had some excellent contract work in his building from the auto industry. He started on-the-job training programs for handicapped people of the area. As work increased, Dave started advertising outside of the city. Handicapped workers were encouraged to provide input of modifications necessary for them to do the jobs correctly. Since adaptive aids usually were not available, Goodwill staff often made their own. With input and ideas from clients, Dave and his staff started writing rehabilitation programs and sharing them with other workshops in the area. Dave soon realized that creating useful material is a time-consuming occupation. In the early 1960's, none, or very little, grant money was available for that purpose. The more programs they developed, the more evident it became that many people needed programs designed for their individual needs.

It was challenging, but rewarding, as they saw people in their 30's, 40's, and 50's becoming wage earners for the first time. The new workers loved telling staff and others, with pride, they were taxpayers. What a change it made in their sense of self worth and in the attitude of their families and friends. Goodwill's staff and Board members started feeling pride in the programs they provided.

Goodwill's workers were blessed when the Board members, who shared Dave's vision, began integrating the workers into their workforce. If on-the-job training was happening at other Goodwills, it wasn't being shared. The Goodwill Industries of America office asked Dave if he would allow staff from other Goodwills to visit the Sandusky facility to observe firsthand what they were doing to change lives. Of course they welcomed them. Staff members from the Ohio Welfare Department also went to visit. Visiting Goodwill executives and supervisors were surprised to hear that Dave and the Sandusky staff were friends with the State employees. Apparently most Goodwills didn't consider their agency as partners with the State employees, but as competitors. Sandusky's Goodwill retail store was also doing well. Goodwill later called from Washington DC, increased the Sandusky territory, and approved Sandusky to be a separate Goodwill.

Dave's daughter Susan, the apple of his eye, was born in Sandusky, Ohio. You will read more about her in other chapters.

CEREAL CITY GOODWILL REHABILITATED

By 1964, as the Sandusky, Ohio Goodwill flourished, it appeared the demise of the Goodwill in Battle Creek, Michigan was near. Civic-minded, caring people, who saw the needs of handicapped persons, founded the Battle Creek Goodwill in 1953. When yet another CEO left the position in 1964, he indicated to Goodwill Industries of America that the Battle Creek organization had so many problems it appeared impossible to get it into a good working order. United Way and other funding sources contacted Goodwill Industries of America to warn of their concerns. Like many of the Goodwills in the 1960's, the Battle Creek Goodwill had no forced rotation for Board members.

Without good leadership in Goodwill's management, members of the board of directors found it difficult to draft qualified men and women Board candidates who were capable of putting new life into the organization. Not wanting to see the organization fail, many of the founding fathers had felt compelled to remain on the Board all those years, with little encouragement from the community. To make matters worse, the staff and clients went out on strike.

In Washington, Goodwill Industries of America (GIA) felt the Battle Creek agency presented a bad image because a Battle Creek staff person contacted a national news agency. Goodwill was the subject of many negative news stories, nation-wide, complete with pictures and quotes. GIA called to ask Dave if he would go to Battle Creek for two or three weeks, and save Goodwill, or close it. When he arrived and reviewed the situation, he called GIA and told them it was just a case of bad management. Joe Pouliot, VP at GIA, told Dave they wanted Goodwill's name to be cleared, and asked him if he would be willing to stay as CEO if he was offered the position. Dave agreed, on the condition that there would be Board rotation, with a limit of two three-year terms. GIA contacted the Executive Committee of the Board; the members were delighted to agree to Dave's request.

Dave met with the Board, then spent the first two weeks talking to Battle Creek's dedicated cash donors to meet payroll, and interviewing every staff member and client. Getting their input on what they perceived to be the strengths and weaknesses of the agency was important to Dave. He hired Ken Shaw as Human Services Director, and competent staff members for other positions, set up a fair compensation package, cleaned up the building and stores, established good staff relations, recruited Board members, and became friends with employees from Michigan Vocational Rehabilitation and other sponsoring agencies.

It was difficult for Dave to get into the Battle Creek building on winter or rainy days. He had to park on a slight incline in the unpaved parking space. A worker had to help him inside. If the elevator had failed when he wasn't on the main floor, he could have been in the Battle Creek building a long time. It became a priority that the building become accessible inside and out to meet the needs of all of their clients.

Every executive director of a Goodwill organization in Michigan became his mentor. He also talked to directors of different types of workshops. In those days, all of them were trying to improve services. It was evident to Dave that he needed all the advice he could get.

Dave, Ken Shaw, and staff members were constantly developing reasonable ways to serve and train employees and clients. Rehabilitation programs were finally dealing with real needs of people with handicaps. Ken developed his own group therapy and behavioral modification classes. These classes were soon shared with other Goodwills and independent workshops.

Chapter 4

There Ought To Be A Law...

WHEN DAVE WAS CEO of Goodwill Industries in Battle Creek during the 60's, money was scarce. Meeting payroll and utilities wasn't easy. Of course Dave wasn't alone. Frank Selleck, a mentor and friend, was the Executive Director of a workshop in Kalamazoo that experienced the same "cashless flow" problem.

Dave always thought a lot of Frank. Frank was one of those distinguished men who always looked the part of a suave, dapper gentleman, competing with Clark Gable. He was noticed when he entered a room. His mustache was always perfectly trimmed, his slacks looked like they had never been sat upon, and his jacket like it had just come out of the cleaner's bag. He wore matching light blue shoes and belt that never had a smudge of dirt on them. He was a man of integrity who cared about people, and did all he could to improve the lifestyle of those less fortunate. Dave and other directors respected him. Like Dave, Frank had a wonderful laugh and smile.

Dave often told our family of the wistful sound in Frank's voice as they discussed a seminar that would be helpful to their agencies. Since the seminar was being offered only once, in the northern part of Michigan's lower-peninsula, the men pondered any possibility of attending. Frank suggested they ride together and share a room to save money.

The planned three-day educational seminar was designed to teach agencies how to serve people with handicaps. Dave appreciated the opportunity to personally meet many of his mentors and State employees he often talked with on the phone. Unfortunately, the person taking reservations had no first-hand knowledge of what "barrier free" or "wheelchair accessible" included. When Dave and Frank arrived, the employee informed them the hotel had run out of barrier free rooms. Their reservation was for a large wheelchair accessible room at a small independent motel.

On the first evening, Dave and Frank left the seminar around 9:30 p.m. Dave often recalled the shock he felt as he pulled into the dark parking lot. He and Frank were speechless. Obviously they were not staying in the most up-to-date motel, but their barrier free room turned out to be a separate little cabin, with no identification except for the faded black number 7 above the door. In that part of the country, the men agreed that it had to be a hunter's cabin.

New snow had covered the tracks of other cars parked in front of the dimly lit rooms. It had been years since the buildings were painted. Huge icicles reached from the roofs to the ground. Dave said nothing, but Frank smiled and asked if the huge icicles held up the cabins' roofs.

It wasn't easy for Frank to get Dave's wheelchair open in the heavy snow. His chair wouldn't have budged if Frank had not tipped the chair back on its big wheels, and pushed Dave slowly to the door. Frank's beautiful slacks and shoes were soaked by the time they arrived. Frank was a little reluctant to put the key into the doorknob and open it. As they entered the ice-cold room, Frank turned on the light, a single 60-watt lightbulb hanging from a cord. Dave's heart sank when he noticed the small bathroom door. When they looked at each other, then around the dimly lit room, Dave said they both wanted to cry. They noticed there wasn't even a phone to call the office. After they had a good laugh, Frank trudged through the unlit parking lot, in deep snow, to the dark corner of the building next door. Obviously, the "No Vacancy" neon sign must belong to the Manager's Office.

Frank's loud, insistent pounding on the door persuaded the unhappy owner to pull himself out of bed and appear at the office door. He was disheveled, resembling Ebenezer Scrooge, in long gray underwear, a red flannel nightshirt, and matching nightcap. He was bewildered because Frank and Dave had not seen the desk chair, which he left for the person in the wheelchair. The person was to transfer to the armless chair and use it to get through the bathroom door. The owner wondered why he and his wife were being awakened so rudely at the ungodly hour of 9:50 p.m. Frank explained the room was ice-cold, and questioned the availability of another room with heat. He said the owner laughed nervously, and assured him that they had the only room available there or anywhere within thirty miles because of the seminar. He insisted they were given the only room with a large barrier-free bathroom doorway. He knew the office chair wouldn't fit through the bathroom doors in the other cabins.

Dave felt sure that Frank's feet must have been freezing before he convinced the owner that they needed heat in the room to be able to sleep. It must have been hard for Frank not to get angry as the owner reluctantly put on a robe and coat, and shuffled through the snow in his slippers to their "barrier-free" room. Although Dave had wrapped a blanket around his shoulders, and a comforter around his legs, his teeth were chattering and his legs ached by the time the man entered their cabin. Dave laughed as he told our grandchildren of the man's scowling and complaining to him about being awakened at such a late hour, as he proceeded to light the burner of the old gas stove. Dave never forgot the threatening sputtering and coughing of the heater.

The sound of the man's shuffling slippers was hardly stilled before Frank was in his bed, pulled the blankets over his head, and was sound asleep. Dave transferred to the freezing "barrier free" seat with no arms, used the bathroom, and went to his bed, fully clothed. He said he felt like the icicles that were hanging from the motel's low roof. He covered up with the comforter and extra blankets. He put the pillows over his head, and lay, hoping to shiver himself to sleep. By the time Dave had settled into his bed, Frank was snoring up a storm. Between listening to his knees knocking from shivering, the stove's noisy threats, and the roaring snoring, Dave finally drifted off to a restless sleep around three or four a.m.

When the alarm clock jolted them awake at 5:30 a.m., the room was up to fifty-five or sixty degrees. Frank's scream from the ice-cold water during a quick shower motivated Dave to shave and wash his face at the hotel. After Dave was safely helped into the car, Frank revisited the unhappy owner and told him he wanted to have warm heat and hot water when they came back that evening. They did.

Dave couldn't think of any other executive attending that meeting who would have laughed at a similar experience. Of course Frank's accurate description of the situation at breakfast caused most of the attendees to roar with laughter. After that experience, Dave always clearly described what a "wheelchair accessible room" is when he made reservations.

At a much later date, after Dave had thawed out, and his frozen state was just a laughable memory, he had to admit that Frank's snoring was a great barrier to his getting a decent night's sleep.

When the seminar was so popular that it was offered again in the summer, in Kalamazoo, Dave and Frank questioned their intelligence at having gone north for a seminar in the winter.

Transferring onto chairs, with or without rollers, with or without arms, from his wheelchair, was a precarious feat which Dave practiced many times during the following years. That was the only "barrier free" that Dave and many of Goodwill's clients knew before Dave helped write State and National Accessibility Laws. The real changes came when Senator Bob Dole completed the Americans with Disability Act (ADA). Thank you Bob! We've come a long way Baby, but there's a long way to go!

Chapter 5

Yes, Michigan Has A Kalamazoo

By 1971, Dave and the staff brought the Battle Creek Goodwill up-to-date. At that time, Lou Arnold, the Board president from Goodwill Industries in Kalamazoo, asked Dave over to advise the Board in their selection of an executive director. Goodwill Industries of America told Lou about Dave's success in the Goodwill branches in Sandusky, Ohio, and Battle Creek, Michigan. Lou told the audience at Dave's 1992 Goodwill Roast that he felt like he had made a big mistake when Dave came into the office. He and the Board members looked at Dave and wondered what this teenage kid with a flattop haircut could tell them about hiring their executive. After Dave shared his vision for their Goodwill, they offered him the job.

The Kalamazoo facility was in the process of being remodeled, and it looked wonderful compared to the one in Battle Creek. One perk that caught Dave's attention was the fact that he would park his company car inside, a few feet from his office; Kalamazoo's building was all on one floor. No more parking on an incline, in a gravel parking space.

Dave told Board members, Lou Arnold and Bill Kirkpatrick, he would accept the Kalamazoo position if there would be Board rotation after two three-year terms. The Board agreed and hired him.

On Dave's first day at the Goodwill facility in Kalamazoo, it was evident that he needed to hire additional qualified staff members. They would be needed to run the state approved rehabilitation program, once it was started. Ken Shaw saved the day when he transferred to Kalamazoo as the Rehabilitation Director. Ken soon gathered some of the best rehabilitation staff any agency had. If they weren't the greatest when he hired them, he soon trained them to be. God seemed to send just the right people for the remaining positions. By the time Dave had been in Kalamazoo eight or nine months, he and Ken knew they had to be able to get out of the building to be able to accomplish their goals.

IT WAS A GOD THING

When people asked Dave how he and I met, Dave told them it was truly a God thing. Dave hoped to become involved outside the office with supporting agencies. He knew that was dependent on his hiring a qualified executive assistant.

When his Human Resources Director placed an ad in the local newspaper, listing all the qualifications needed for the position, there were many responses, but no qualified applicants.

Dave called all employment agencies listed in the Kalamazoo phone book to find a qualified applicant. Several of them laughed on the phone when they learned what his expectations for the position were, and what he could pay. Most recruiters confessed that if they had anyone who met his expectations, they would place them with a high-paying employer. When they learned Goodwill could not pay the finder's fee, the recruiters wished him luck.

A few days later, Dave received a call. The woman calling explained she was from a recruiting agency, new to the area. She said her agency had just gotten a resume that sounded like the perfect candidate for his advertised position, so she was following up to see if the position had been filled. Dave had not called her agency because it wasn't in the phone book. After they talked, the recruiter hand-carried the resume to Goodwill for Dave to read. After he read it, he knew God found him the right person! The recruiter used Dave's office phone, and called the phone number listed on the resume.

In 1972, I was the church secretary at Oakland Drive Christian Church. The minister and church leadership were easy to work for, and I had ideal hours.

A church member came in to volunteer the day before the recruiter called, and told me that she needed my job. That night I had a recurring dream that I should seek another job. I argued with the Lord, and told Him that I wouldn't look for another job. If He wanted me to leave, He would have to have someone call me with a job offer. My new boss would have to be as fine a Christian, with a great sense of humor and a laugh as sincere, as our pastor.

While I sat praying at my desk the next morning, the phone rang. The woman on the other line told me that my resume had just surfaced on her desk that morning, and that she had the perfect job for me. I was surprised at her statement, but knew God was involved. I let her know I hadn't updated my resume in over six years and had never sent a resume to an employment agency. I rudely told her I wasn't interested in her position. She ignored my comment, and said she was with Mr. David Davey, the CEO at Goodwill Industries. She said he had read my resume, and was interested in interviewing me. She flattered me by saying I would be perfect for his Executive Assistant position. I told her I was not interested in sorting clothes or working in a store. She laughed and told me I wouldn't be doing either. She explained what my duties would be, and then added that Mr. Davey was a strong Christian. It was obvious God had heard my prayer. I finally agreed to go for an interview the following morning if Mr. Davey would interview me at 7:00 a.m. so I could be at the church by 8:30 a.m. He agreed.

The next morning, a very tall young woman, who identified herself as the human resources director, met me at the door with a big smile. I followed her through a maze of framed in, unfinished rooms, to a table in the hallway outside her office. She told me that Mr. Davey would be in shortly so she would give me a battery of tests until he arrived. Since I had only agreed to an interview, I was pretty disgusted but finished the tests ahead of time. She was surprised when I scored 100 percent on all of them. I explained that I still wasn't interested in the job. By that time, I was getting pretty angry because Mr. Davey had not shown up. The human resources director wanted me to take a fifteen-minute typing test, but she promised me that I would stop when Mr. Davey arrived. The typewriter was an old manual. At church I had a new, long carriage electric typewriter. I told her I always freeze up on typing tests, and had been assured I would not have to take one. She reminded me that I didn't want the job, so I really didn't have anything to lose. Her original had many errors in it. I corrected the errors, but I'm sure I typed worse than I ever had on a typing test.

After I had finished typing, the human resources director told me she felt I'd be perfect for the job. I told her I appreciated her coming in early, but I wasn't interested in the position. After giving her several reasons, I noticed it was 8:00 a.m. I let her know I certainly didn't care to work for someone who didn't keep his appointments. She was apologetic as she walked me to the door, and told me she would call me later. I told her not to bother. If I didn't get a call personally from Mr. Davey, explaining his failure to keep his word, I wouldn't even take the call. I jumped into my car and drove, fuming, to church. By the time I arrived, I was convinced God was not going to make me take that job.

As I entered the church, the phone was ringing. It was Mr. Davey who apologized and said he just missed me. He said he was driving into the garage as I was leaving the parking lot. The HR director tried to stop me when she saw his car, but I was already gone. He apologized and told me he wished he could tell me a story about a car breakdown or a bad accident, but it didn't happen. He left his home in Battle Creek at five thirty and decided to drive around Gull Lake to pray about the interview on his way to work. When he got lost, it took longer than he planned.

Since I get lost easily, I laughed and told him I also like to drive different routes when I have something special to pray about. I remember being angry with myself for being so supportive of his actions. He asked me if I could return immediately for the interview. The nerve of the guy! I told him, most sarcastically, I had a very busy day, and would only agree to come the next morning if he promised me he would be at the door, at 7 a.m., to greet me. I told him if he wasn't, I wouldn't even enter the building, but would get back into my car and leave. He assured me he would be there.

As I drove to the interview, I tried to convince myself to give weird answers so Mr. Davey wouldn't consider me for the position. I prayed that God wouldn't make me take that job for several reasons. I tried to convince God that the church needed the skills He had given me. I could tell God was ignoring me. When I got out of the car, I didn't see anyone standing in the doorway, only a young man nineteen or twenty sitting outside in a wheelchair. The sliding door was open. I figured the young man was a client, but decided to go in, just in case Mr. Davey was around the corner, talking to him. As I went up the steps, I smiled at the young man. He smiled and introduced himself as David Davey. I was surprised and told him I wasn't expecting anyone so young, or in a wheelchair. He asked if it would bother me to work for someone younger or in a wheelchair. I assured him it wouldn't if he could do his job. He laughed, and said that was the answer he wanted to hear, and asked me to call him Dave. Later I learned he was sixteen months older than I.

As I followed him to his humble office, I remember thinking, "Oh no, his laugh is just like my pastor's. Lord, what are you doing to me?"

Dave said he laughed when he was told about my resistance to taking the typing test. Although my typing test wasn't great, I had corrected all of the misspelled words and grammatical errors purposely placed on the typing test. When Dave was told that I had perfect scores on all the written tests, he was impressed.

When I told him I might be moving to Indianapolis in a year or two if my plans required it, he later said he figured I was saying that to discourage him from hiring me. He felt confident that if we worked together for two years, we would get the office and staff organized. Goodwill needed to be accredited by the Commission on Accreditation of Rehabilitation Facilities (CARF) to be able to receive government funds. At the time of my interview, there was no written material in the facility. Dave was confident that I could write the manuals, job descriptions, etc., necessary for the required accreditation.

I couldn't believe it, but there I was telling Dave that I actually typed eighty or ninety words a minute accurately. I felt like I was a stranger listening in on the interview. Dave shared the dreams and plans that he and Dick Wooten, his roommate at Wayne State University, had in the 1950's. He told me that he felt it was his destiny to make life easier for individuals with handicaps. Properly trained Goodwill staff could make a difference by assisting clients in preparation for employment. When he told me how he and Ken Shaw planned to bring those dreams to fruition, I was in agreement that it was possible. Dave was certain that legislation was needed to assist with his planned endeavors. A partner was needed so he could pursue these dreams. I sat on the edge of my chair, arms on his desk, nodding approval as he shared their plans for the Kalamazoo Goodwill. I was enthralled at the possibility of being a part of this life-changing team. I found myself asking many questions, and telling him about my skills, and how I felt I could help the team.

Dave complimented me on my quick smile, and told me that he felt a good sense of humor was important to people who wanted to help people. My thoughts exactly! We were both amazed about how much we had in common. He said he appreciated the professional way I was dressed, that I walked like I had confidence in myself, that I had the courage to speak my mind, yet wasn't prejudiced, and I impressed him because I looked him straight in the eyes during the entire interview. He said his assistant needed those attributes because of the varied duties of the position. He was so easy to talk to that time seemed to fly. His laugh was hearty when he said he was ecstatic when he called me and I chewed him out. He knew I would keep him in line, on time, and he felt I was perfect for the job. I was sorry when I had to leave, and was singing as I drove to the church.

The phone was ringing as I entered the church. It was another woman from the same recruiting office. She told me she had an Office Manager position available at a successful local business. The company offered an excellent starting salary and benefits. The company was willing to pay the twelve-hundred-dollar finder's fee as well. She asked if the owner could interview me that day. I told her I would be available if he or she was willing to meet me after 4:30 p.m. She called back and said anytime between 4:30 and 6:00 p.m. would be fine with the owner. I really wondered what the Lord had put on the resume of mine that I had never seen.

I barely hung up when Dave was on the phone, offering me the position at Goodwill. I told him I enjoyed the interview, but explained about the salary and perks I was being offered at the other company. I reminded him that I had forgotten to ask him what the job at Goodwill paid. He was quiet for a few seconds before he told me he made about half of what I was being offered at the other company. The Goodwill job paid ninety dollars a week, with benefits. When I told him that the other business would pay the twelve-hundred-dollar finder's fee, he said he was sorry, but Goodwill couldn't pay the one-hundred-dollars finder's fee for their position. I told him I'd have to pray about this since there was such a difference in pay and incentives.

I arrived at the other company a little early, and the owner immediately took me into his lovely office. He asked me a few questions, smiled, nodded, and then took me into a large room with several women and a ticker tape. He asked me to check the ticker tape and tell him what I felt it meant. I looked at it, smiled, and told him it looked like we were making a profit today. He said, "I knew you'd say 'we' because you're a team player." All the women smiled and told me they hoped I'd take the job. We returned to the owner's office. He handed me a typed copy of his employment offer, and asked when I could start. I looked at the amazing offer, and told him I would have to go home and pray about it overnight because I was considering an offer from Mr. Davey at Goodwill. He was shocked, and asked if Goodwill could match his offer. I laughed when I assured him they couldn't come close. I promised I'd call him at 10 a.m. the next day with my decision. He told me that he and all the girls hoped that I'd accept his offer.

I prayed all the way home, telling myself that this job was a fabulous opportunity, with less than half the miles it was to Goodwill. I'd have a company car, and I tried to convince God and myself that the extra money would mean I could save faster to move to Indianapolis. Actually, I had forgotten about wanting to leave Kalamazoo after my interview with Mr. Davey. All night long I prayed. Before I even went to bed, I knew God wanted me to be a partner with Dave, assisting him, so he could develop the programs we discussed.

The next morning, when I called Dave, and heard his cheerful voice on the other end of the line, I felt like I'd known him all my life. When I greeted him, I loved his response. I told him I had argued with the Holy Spirit all night, praising God for the wonderful opportunity He gave me for both jobs. I could tell Dave thought I had decided to accept the other offer. I told him that maybe I was being foolish but I felt that God wanted me to be his partner, assisting in making his lifetime dream of helping people become a reality. He was quiet for a few seconds, and then shouted something like, "Praise the Lord." I laughed and told him he might have other thoughts after I worked for him for five years. He reminded me of my statement when we were married five years later.

He confided that he had asked members of the Battle Creek Bible Church to pray that God would send him someone who would say he or she wanted to be a partner with him in developing programs. When I heard that, I knew I was in the Lord's will for my life.

I tried to contact the recruiting service several months later to hire a printer; the Michigan Bell Telephone operator told me there was no such number. Out of curiosity, I drove to the address on the business card, only to recognize that it belonged to the Social

Security office who had been at that address for years. Dave was right! It had to be a God thing.

TEAMWORK

As soon as they had their staff on board, Dave and Ken Shaw spent time developing a team that shared their vision. Their team goal was to change lives at the local Goodwill as well as elsewhere. By sharing their knowledge, they hoped all handicapped people in America could benefit from what their team was able to accomplish.

The pace was very fast as Dave and Ken were busily making their goals a reality. Staff members were working much harder as part of the team than they would have been asked to work at another agency. Fortunately, all of the team members were dedicated to making a difference in lives, and had a great sense of humor. Dave and Ken gave everyone the opportunity to develop his or her position. They encouraged the staff to expand their parameters so they could better help others. Programs were constantly improving. The staff didn't complain, but said having the freedom to be creative made the extra work seem like fun. The team shared every accomplishment with everyone, encouraging each other. If a new staff member wasn't a team player, he or she didn't choose to stay very long. People with the same vision pursued the success of all the programs.

BOARD MEMBERS

Members of our board of directors consisted of many caring people. Most members were men and women of integrity. They wanted our clients and programs to succeed; they drew upon other professionals to support their effort. Most of them shared Dave's vision. They used their influence to help expand services to our clients, and to improve equipment in the offices, stores, and manufacturing areas. These wonderful men and women made Dave's job and that of our staff members more fruitful. They were an inspiration to us.

Dave, Ken, and the staff members became partners with many of the board members. Together they helped develop Work Experience programs that were soon being utilized with contract work provided by the board members' employers. They also talked to their friends. Companies began to create positions so our clients could receive job training in their facilities. Several board members came, or had their employees come, to our facility to help develop workstations for jobs provided by many local companies.

NEW SERVICES

Soon Goodwill's local office and their programs were running smoothly. Dave started getting more involved with the many rehabilitation agencies that could help Goodwill. He was soon an officer in many of them. Dave, Ken and the staff helped develop programs to assist clients at Goodwill and other agencies. We became involved in working with Michigan Services for the Blind.

As Michigan Services for the Blind staff members listen, Dave accidentally holds, upside down, the plaque he received for Outstanding Work with Blind Clients, Dave and the blind staff thought laughter was because of his speech. No one said anything until they showed him the picture.

I wrote job descriptions, program manuals, procedural manuals, inspection manuals, and anything else that was a requirement of the Commission on Accreditation of Rehabilitation Facilities (CARF). Our Goodwill shared these new detail-oriented manuals with other agencies. It helped those agencies to expand their services and be accredited faster. The national, state, and local organizations where Dave was an officer or committee chair usually needed help. Faded copies of hand written notes were often the norm when he joined organizations. Dave's typed, well written paperwork for committees helped bring a professional expectation from members of other organizations when he was an officer for them. Serving on many committees was keeping Dave away from the office more and more. Our Goodwill soon received an excellent rating from the Commission on Accreditation of Rehabilitation Facilities.

By 1974, it was becoming difficult for Michigan Goodwills to contract with State agencies. It soon became apparent that Michigan had no organization available for staff of facilities providing vocational rehabilitation, sheltered workshops and activity centers to share information or act collectively on matters of mutual interest. They had no voice representing their needs to State agencies. Everyone seemed to be blindly competing with each other for State funds. Dave and Ken Shaw discussed with friends at Michigan Vocational Rehabilitation Services (MRS) what this Goodwill could do to turn a lose-lose situation into a win-win situation for everyone involved. MRS agreed it would be to their advantage if they were able to compare "apples to apples" when they decided what agencies could best serve individual clients. In turn, Dave and Ken Shaw agreed to furnish copies of our Goodwill's programs to any organization that needed them. Every agency in Michigan gladly accepted.

When Dave communicated with top management of every Goodwill and other workshops in Michigan to discuss the need to organize, Dave decided to take the initiative to remedy this situation. I believe it was in 1974 that Dave solicited the assistance of Michigan Goodwill CEOs Ken Gonser of Adrian, Gerry

Kane of Flint, and Del Wisecarver of Detroit, in establishing the Michigan Association of Rehabilitation Facilities (MARF) for the purpose of providing high quality programs of rehabilitation for handicapped individuals.

Members of the Michigan Vocational Rehabilitation Services and Michigan Blind Services met many times at our local Goodwill to assist in this new agency development. The newly formed MARF team members were able to secure a grant from Michigan's Bureau of Vocational Rehabilitation to hire the first executive director of MARF. The current name of the agency is MARO Employment and Training Association. Dave was on the original board of directors for eight years, and served as treasurer for two years. Until he suffered respiratory failure in 1989, I believe Dave attended every MARF meeting.

In 1977, Dave became the first Goodwill executive invited to serve on the board of directors of the Commission on Accreditation of Rehabilitation Facilities (CARF). He served two terms. He was a member of the committee to review and revise the Commission's bylaws; he also served as vice-chairman of the board.

Finally, "handicap" was no longer considered a stigma you had to whisper about. Dave served on many committees, including: the Traumatically Brain Injured Planning Task Force, Local Building Code Committee, Transportation Advisory Council of Kalamazoo, Employment Planning Committee of Kalamazoo County Mental Health, Department of Social Services project for general assistance recipients, Advisory Council for Kalamazoo Valley Community College, State Advisory Council for the Michigan State Technical Institute and Rehabilitation Center, State of Michigan Vocational Rehabilitation Advisory Council, and many others. Dave and Ken Shaw made a commitment to become personally involved with everyone who could help our cause. If Dave wasn't on a committee, it was because Ken Shaw was a member, often an officer. Goodwill Industries of Southwestern Michigan was finally being recognized as an agency that changed lives.

Dave became personal friends with many of the leaders of agencies, colleges, and companies with whom Goodwill was involved. He had great respect for Dr. Dale Lake, the founding president of Kalamazoo Valley Community College. Dave appreciated each time Dr. Lake called him from Florida after his retirement. They discussed some of their dream projects they shared for this community. By the time Dave retired, they were pleased that most of their dreams were a reality.

Dave wrote letters to legislators, media, etc., and worked with every group he could to eliminate all barriers he saw. From the time he began using a wheelchair at twelve, Dave saw many needs that went unnoticed by people able to walk. The sidewalk curbs sometimes were as high as twelve or sixteen inches, with no corner cuts; toilet doors in public places were impossible for wheelchairs to enter; most house bathroom doors wouldn't facilitate a wheelchair. The list went on and on. If there was a committee that needed input from a wheelchair user, Dave was soon a member.

As a result, he was invited to be a member of the National Architectural Barrier and Transportation Board, serving with Senator Bob Dole. Dave had always respected Senator Dole so that was a wonderful experience. Senator Dole and the NABT board members were anxious to make a difference in the national laws. National buildings, monuments, etc. soon became wheelchair accessible.

Although the desire was discussed at several meetings, Dave and the committee felt airline toilet doors will always be impossible for people confined to wheelchairs to use because the wheelchairs are put in the bottom of the plane with the luggage. On long trips, I held up a blanket while Dave drained his urinal into a jar in my carrying case. I emptied it in the plane toilet.

On the Michigan Building Code Commission—Barrier Free Design Board, Dave was finally able to help influence laws and regulations for accessibility to public buildings, monuments, restrooms, doorways and curb cuts for walks, streets, etc. for people in Michigan. It became a law that restrooms in buildings available to the public, i.e. hotels, motels, restaurants, theatres, etc., built after the laws went into effect, had to provide at least one wheelchair accessible toilet in every restroom. The buildings were required to have a designated number of wheelchair accessible rooms, parking spaces, etc. Dave felt driven to educate employees of local, state and national organizations on how to assist their communities. They needed to be aware of their responsibility to the handicapped.

Dave organized teams of TV, radio, and newspaper staff to accompany him to inspect new buildings in Kalamazoo County for compliance to the laws. Goodwill furnished wheelchairs for them to sit on during the inspection. When the person using the wheelchair entered a restroom through a large, unobstructed door, they were shocked on their way out when they experienced a large, heavy wastebasket that had been placed in a small corner and blocked half of the door, it was obvious that a wheelchair user couldn't pass through the available space, and was helpless to move the wastebasket. Cameras rolled. Some discovered they couldn't wash their hands because they were unable to reach the faucets, etc. Soon a large campaign spread throughout Kalamazoo County. Local residents couldn't pick up a newspaper, or turn on a radio or TV without seeing that the media was helping make this new law known. TV crews visited restrooms of many companies. It might have taken years if they hadn't been so cooperative. Dave sent copies of all articles to every Goodwill CEO, and suggested they talk to their local media. He received letters thanking him, and sharing what other Goodwills were doing in their locations. Goodwills made a difference!

After a newspaper article discussed the new laws, and told of Dave's involvement with them, he was surprised at how many people thanked him because of the curb cuts. Wheelchair users loved them; parents could now use their strollers and buggies on sidewalks without having to lift them up or down when they came to a street to cross. Their families used the cuts while bicycle and tricycle riding, skating, etc. Before the cuts, the only way Dave could go into businesses downtown was to park close enough to the sidewalk to open the passenger side of his car, remove his chair from the backseat, and still be able to pull himself onto his chair on the sidewalk, as he exited the passenger side of the car. It's hard to think that in 1960, people using battery powered riding chairs and scooters couldn't have gotten off the sidewalk to cross the street because of the high curbs. Most permanent wheelchair users cannot stand on their feet and legs, thus making them dependent on their shoulders and arms to move.

Storeowners soon took pride in their handicapped parking spaces. The media interviewed them and complimented them in the paper or on air. Businesses called Goodwill to locate suppliers of wheelchair signs, directions, etc. Restaurants and other businesses began calling Dave to tell him when they made their restrooms accessible, or when they added extra wheelchair parking spaces. They asked him to inspect them. He often had a TV, radio, or newspaper representative to accompany him. The restaurants told Dave that the publicity helped their business. Things were finally moving at a positive and fast pace.

At first, many drivers ignored the wheelchair signs, and mocked anyone who said anything to them. When interviewed by TV employees about being parked in the areas without a special license or card, violators cursed them or used vulgar language. The TV stations put the footage of their comments on the six and eleven o'clock news. It didn't take long, with the media's help, for informed civic-minded citizens or employees who saw illegally parked cars to call the police. Police began giving tickets. Drivers who ignored the parking tickets were soon convinced the law was here to stay when they came out and found their vehicle had been towed.

Dave talked at meetings of local, statewide, and national architects to encourage them to discontinue building anything with small doorways, especially bathrooms. He encouraged them to design and build ramps according to code, in addition to the steps to entranceways. When he spoke, he could tell the audience, very convincingly, how frightening it had been for him when he was carried up steps to churches, restaurants, hotels and private homes. He explained the inconvenience to chair users, caused by steps, sunken rooms, or a high threshold. He personally called architects when he learned they had a family member using a chair. Most were willing participants when he asked them to accompany him and to speak at the meetings. Some of the architects' stories about family members' experiences were even more frightening than Dave's.

Most architects in the audience were cooperative, and glad they could help. When the hotel was being built in downtown Kalamazoo, Dave wrote to the general contractor. Dave explained that he knew of many organizations that would utilize the facility if there were enough wheelchair accessible rooms to facilitate their members. The contractor told Dave they would attempt to make all bathroom doors accessible.

Dave, Dick Wooten, Dave's college roommate, and Goodwill execs across America, began using their legislators to bring about results. It was happening!

What a difference the Americans with Disabilities Act (ADA), that came later, has made in America and much of the world.

SMILE AND THE WHOLE WORLD SMILES WITH YOU

To keep positive under the fast pace we were working, a good sense of humor was important to Dave, his staff and Board. At a board meeting, Dave was proudly explaining that our Goodwill had received funding for a new program to serve the hearing impaired. After he explained the program in its entirety, a new board member cupped his ear and asked, "What was that you said, David?" Thinking he hadn't been clear in his explanation, Dave once again explained the program in its entirety. Again the board member asked, "I'm sorry, but what was that you said, David?" None of the Board members cracked a smile. Before Dave could say anything, I said, "Mr. Davey, I think that's called an 'I gotcha!'" The board members roared, and Dave turned crimson.

WHAT GOES AROUND, COMES AROUND

I gotcha!! Those two words took on a new meaning in the 1970's. Upon my return to work from a vacation, there was a small loving cup on my desk. Assuming it was for pencils and belonged to my assistant, I took it to her. Complete innocence enveloped her as she denied ownership, and suggested I look for some means of identification on the cup.

Sure enough, on the bottom was a cartoon cutout of a woman with wire rimmed granny glasses, sagging cotton stockings, granny shoes, an old fashioned house dress, and straight, straggly hair topped with a small pill box hat that was adorned by a bent, artificial flower. She was sitting with her legs spread apart, while her boss stood at a podium, making the statement, "...and now, let's hear it for my secretary." The wheels began to spin. I knew I'd been had. I complimented Dave on the likeness and thanked him in my most sincere voice. His halo was badly tilted as he feigned ignorance of the cup.

The next morning a candidate for the board of directors was scheduled for an interview at 10:00 a.m. When Dorothy Haynes, the chairman of the Nominating Committee, nominated him for the board, she told the members what a great sense of humor he had, and what a great addition to the Board he would be. She urged everyone to make him feel welcome at the Annual Meeting so he would accept the nomination.

A great sense of humor! What an opportunity! At 9:30 a.m., I asked my assistant to meet the board candidate when he arrived at 10:00 a.m., and take him to Dave's office because I had a meeting to attend. I told her I would be back in time to get them coffee. I removed my makeup, took my loving cup, then hurried to the donated goods area and let the supervisor in on my strategy.

She knew she could make me look like the drawing, but questioned my sanity if I wanted to look like that. We compared the likeness on the cup to items available in different areas. Out of Halloween costumes came the perfect black, straight human hair wig; the dress we pulled out of the baler was two or three sizes too large, and almost identical to the one in the picture; on the floor was a pair of brown cotton full length stockings that I had to pin to my panties, loose enough that they were baggy at the ankles; we chose shoes from the compactor—men's golf shoes without the cleats—right size, right look; from glasses saved for the Lions Club came the small wire rims with no glass; we found the perfect small round, brown felt hat, and off the floor I found the bent, yellow flower to stick on top. The supervisor ran the wig, dress and socks through the dryer. After the dress was pressed, she combed the wig on me, and I was on my way to meet the new candidate.

The workers in the clothing area felt we had accomplished a perfect makeover. As I passed a mirror on my return to the office at 10:05, I was a dead ringer of the recipient on the bottom of my cup. When my assistant saw me, she nearly choked on her peanut butter sandwich.

The board candidate and Dave were safely locked in his office when I picked up my phone and asked in my most businesslike voice, "May I get you two a cup of coffee?"

"Yes, both black," was music to my ears. It was with a bland face and voice that I delivered the coffee and asked if there was anything else that I could get them. The candidate had a cheerful smile, and looked casual in his sweater vest over a white shirt. His eyes nearly bugged out of his head as he gave me the twice over, and Dave calmly introduced us. As the man shook my limp hand, Dave didn't say a word.

I quickly left, changed my clothes, redid my hair and stayed hidden until the candidate left the building. At 11:00 a.m. I met the next candidate in a most professional manner. Dave later said neither he nor the man he interviewed at 10:00 a.m. had said a word about me after I'd left the room. Both candidates told Dave they would be happy to serve on the Board.

Two or three weeks later, I had forgotten all about the interview as I was standing with some board members, greeting everyone at the annual meeting. I had my natural strawberry blond hair done up in a fashionable upsweep, and was wearing a beautiful full-length, size ten, fitted white formal, with long sleeves and a high neckline. My makeup was perfect. All of the board members and staff had complimented me on how great I looked.

As I was intermingling with the crowd, I saw Dorothy Haynes standing at the entranceway, talking to a nicely dressed couple for quite some time. I could tell they were good friends because, as they were laughing, Dorothy had her right hand resting on the woman's shoulder. I didn't recognize the man nor the woman. Suddenly, several other guests entered the door, and went toward Dorothy.

The nicely dressed couple left Dorothy's side, came up to me, looked around, and the man quietly asked me where Mr. Davey's executive assistant was. Before I could reply, he introduced himself as a board candidate, and told me he could hardly wait for his wife to meet Dave's assistant. His wife spoke up and said Dorothy Haynes and her husband told her how efficient Mr. Davey's assistant was. I hadn't recognized him in his suit, but I almost choked when I recognized his voice; and it dawned on me which candidate he was.

We became close friends after I shared with them the "other woman" he had met. He was still laughing as he turned around, and told his wife he knew he was going to love being on this board if he was elected. His wife gave me a big hug and, after she was able to quit laughing and had regained her composure, she told me her husband would never forget that interview. I pointed out where Dave was sitting. A short time later, I heard him say, "Dave, I think Anne gotcha!" Before the evening was over, the story was known by most of the board members.

MORE HAPPENED THAT NIGHT...

I'll never forget that night. So much happened! It was the first time Dave's mom and stepfather met me. It had only been two weeks since Dave had proposed. Dave had told them how he felt about me, but they had no idea what I looked like.

Dave with his parents Bill and Helen Simpson outside restaurant
after he told them he had asked me to marry him.

They had agreed to come to Kalamazoo, from Sterling Heights, Michigan, to Goodwill's annual meeting. Dave had registered them and paid for their tickets, but neglected to mention their coming to anyone. I had never seen a picture of them.

A short time after the candidate shared his story with Dorothy Haynes, she and I returned to the entranceway to greet the last few guests. We were still laughing when Dave's parents arrived. After Dorothy and I welcomed them, I offered to get their nametags. They came with me, and introduced themselves as Bill and Helen Simpson. I didn't recognize their names.

They told me they wanted to surprise Mr. Davey's secretary. They asked me to point her out. They were looking around the room as they talked. Before I could say anything, Bill Kirkpatrick, a former board president and husband of the current board president, came over and told them that Dave had sent him over to bring them to the area where he was. Dave didn't tell Bill who they were. There were several female staff members standing around Dave in preparation for the meeting to begin. Dave's parents looked at every woman as we walked toward Dave.

Still looking around, Mom asked Dave if Anne was there so they might meet her. The board president, Fran Kirkpatrick, tapped Dave on the shoulder, and reminded him the meeting should begin. Although I was standing next to them, Dave turned around and told his parents he would introduce them after the meeting was over. I still had no idea who they were.

Since they appeared to be Dave's friends, Bill Kirkpatrick and I invited them to sit with us at the table in front of the head table. When I started taking minutes of the meeting, Dave's mom asked Bill Kirkpatrick what he thought of Anne. He told her that David was the envy of a lot of his single friends. I nearly choked, listening to their conversation about me.

The guest speaker that evening was Harold Wilke, a man who was born without arms. He was a real pioneer in the world of rehabilitation; Dave highly respected his contributions. That afternoon Harold asked me to repair a hole in one of his toe socks. While sitting at the head table during the meeting, he got everyone's attention when he picked up a ladle with his right foot, and poured the salad dressing on Fran's salad, without spilling a drop. After the meeting, he stood on his left foot as he shook the hands of guests with his right foot.

On the day of the Annual Meeting, I typed out the script for the "Volunteer of the Year" award. At that time, our communications director indicated the winner was going to be the president of the Auxiliary. At the meeting, she described many of the volunteer's impressive accomplishments. It was obvious she wasn't following the script I had typed. I was taking notes when she announced, "This year's "Volunteer of the Year is David Davey's Executive Assistant, Anne." Dave's parents were looking around.

I sat there waiting for the Auxiliary president to go on stage. Bill Kirkpatrick leaned over and said, "Anne, it's you." As I went up to the head table, still in a daze, Dave's parents were shocked to know they had been sitting next to me all that time. Dave was also unaware that I was going to be receiving this award, given by the Board Communications Committee.

That evening, after the meeting, Dave introduced his parents and me. We went over to Dave's apartment to get acquainted. Fortunately, his parents liked me. His mom told Dave what Bill Kirkpatrick had said. She warned him to be careful or he might lose me. His dad, mom, and I laughed, but Dave wasn't smiling when he told us that Bill Kirkpatrick had asked him earlier if he was interested in me because some of his friends wanted to meet me. Dave told me years later he had been jealous, and feared that I might be interested in the richer men that were Bill's friends. I told Dave that that fear was hilarious; because I knew there was no one better than Dave.

Chapter 6

Our Posterity

This chapter was written by Dave shortly before his death.

SUSAN

MY WONDERFUL DAUGHTER Susan was born in 1963, in Sandusky, Ohio. I was out in the waiting room when she was handed to me. She opened her eyes and smiled at me. That had to be the happiest moment of my twenty-seven years. I praised God for her; I was so proud to be a dad that I wanted to tell the world. If I could have walked, I would have jumped up and clicked my heels. Susan was a baby when we moved to Battle Creek. She was so precious I spent every minute I could with her.

Susan grew up so fast. When she was still a baby, she would hide behind our fireplace and play peek-a-boo when I'd come home. She'd laugh and laugh. As soon as she could walk, she had a habit of eating the lint out of the dryer, and loved to tease me with the leftovers. She looked so precious when she'd turn her head toward me with the lint hanging out of her mouth. She loved having her picture taken. She'd often pose with her hands on her hips, and her eyes dancing as if to challenge me to try some of the lint. I looked forward to the times I could take her for rides to see animals in the fields. We visited zoos, parks, Bird Sanctuary, Kellogg's Farm, and farms of friends and family. It was wonderful to be able to watch her growing up so quickly. When we went down to Frankfort, Indiana, Uncle Walter took her out to the chicken coop and let her gather eggs. She loved pumping well-water into the bucket.

Susan Davey pumping water for Uncle Walter's farm animals

Susan could hardly wait for winter so she could go down the hills at the Arboretum in Battle Creek on her sled. Afterward, she got into the car, full of snow, laughing as she told me how her stomach felt as she zoomed down the hill and came to the sudden stops. I took pictures from the car of her descent, but I wish I had taken pictures of her inside the car. Her eyes were so expressive, and her cheeks a rosy pink. What a delight!

Susan and her sled after going downhill at Battle Creek Arboretum

Susan and I had a fun game, "Brighten the corner where you are," that we sang every night. We also sang, "This little light of mine." I flashed the light into all corners of her room so she wouldn't be afraid. We'd sing together and laugh so hard. I love that memory.

When Susan was young, I had an occasion to reflect back to the time when I was little and my family moved to a new home. Mom was busy inside, arranging the furniture, and I was out in the yard getting to know the neighborhood children. Within twenty minutes Mom heard a terrible ruckus in the front yard. There I was, beating the tar out of a kid. Mom came running out, apparently embarrassed, and asking me, "David, what are you thinking? We haven't even moved in, and here you are beating up the neighborhood children." She said I innocently declared, "I had to do it Mom because he cussed on my property." Even though I beat up the kids who swore in our yard, I must have remembered the terminology they used. On a spring day, several months later, Mom got a phone call from my teacher. After talking with Mom for over a half hour, the teacher told her, "We've been talking for over a half hour and you haven't even said 'darn' once." When Mom asked her if she should have, the teacher said, "Your son has quite a mouth." When she shared some of the words I had been overheard repeating, Mom quickly assured her, "I can promise you that you won't be bothered with that mouth again." I gave up that part of my vocabulary that evening.

Years later, when we lived in Battle Creek, I wondered if this could have been hereditary. I was having my hair cut when my barber asked if Susan Davey was my daughter, and I proudly said, "Yes." The barber told me about the foul language that Susan was shouting at the adults in the neighborhood. Remembering the discussion I had experienced with Mom many years before, I had the same little talk with Susan, and she also gave up that part of her vocabulary. Mom's eyes danced as she reminded me, "The apple doesn't fall far from the tree."

I called Susan my little Woozer. It was very special to both of us. I assisted Anne's children, Julie and David, and their friends in making a large four feet high sign stating, "HAPPY BIRTHDAY WOOZER." They put it across the front of Anne's house when they had a party for Susan's twelfth or thirteenth birthday. Sometime that year, David saved his money to take Susan to Red Lobster. They were good friends.

I still remember how thrilled Susan was when Julie, David and other friends TP'd our yard and house. Julie told me they had been on the back porch, preparing to wrap the doorway with toilet paper when the back door was opened to let out Susan's dog, Muffin. When Muffin started barking, we called her back into the house because we thought she saw an animal. She was making so much noise, and it was so late; we didn't want to disturb the neighbors. The next day Susan thought it was wonderful when she saw toilet paper wrapped around the house, trees, bushes, and outside furniture. She felt so grown up because, in those days, it was considered a status symbol, and it only happened to the most popular kids in school. She could hardly wait to tell her classmates.

I'm so proud of Susan. She has a wonderful voice and took singing lessons with a teacher from Kalamazoo College. Once, she and her friends sang on Channel 3 TV. Susan was in the play

"Oklahoma" in high school. She was an honor student in high school and college. She often sings solos at church. She worked at the Portage Library. She was a candy striper at Bronson Hospital. When she was still in high school, Susan decided she wanted to be an occupational therapist.

Western Michigan University accepted Susan in their Occupational Therapy program. She chose to begin classes immediately out of high school. Before her last semester at WMU, Susan visited her best girlfriend who was stationed at a US Air Force base in Germany. They traveled in Europe. After returning home, she interned in Lansing and at Croyden School in Kalamazoo. Upon graduation, she worked at Bronson Medical Center.

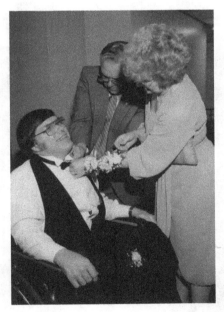

Stan Zidel and Anne Davey help tie Dave's bow tie for Susan and James wedding

Shortly after her graduation, I proudly rode down the aisle beside Susan, and gave her away in marriage to James Gibson. What a beautiful bride. What a great man James is.

*John and Anna Eley and Aunt Ella with Dave
Davey at Susan & James wedding*

Susan and James Gibson with Grandma Simpson on their wedding day

Susan and James were married several years before they had their three wonderful children, Maegan, Jessica and Joshua, all artistic and possessing a great sense of humor.

Grandparents Bill and Beth Gibson, and Dave and Anne Davey, celebrate Maegan's dedication with James (holding Maegan), and Susan Gibson

When Maegan was a baby, Susan continued working as an Occupational Therapist on week-ends so James and Maegan had a chance to bond. After Jessica's birth, Susan worked for a short time and decided to be a stay-at-home Mom.

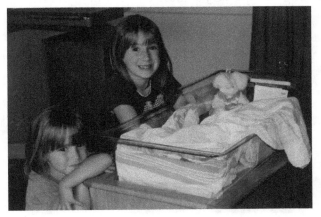

Maegan and Jessica are proud sisters of newborn brother Joshua

Although they live in the same city as we, their family is very busy so we don't get to see them as often as we'd like.

Four generations—Great Grandmother Helen Simpson, Maegan and Jessica, Mom Susan Gibson, and proud Grandpa David Davey

Anne and I often take the children to McDonald's where they enjoy the inside playground after we eat. When Anne is speaking at retreats, I often drive the grandchildren to see animals in the country, then to lunch or dinner. We look forward to the children coming overnight. After dinner we play board games and have tea parties, using the special Japanese tea set I bought Anne.

Maegan, Anne, Dave, Jessica, and Susan have a birthday party at Bill Knapps

What I love best is watching them become young adults, and hearing their opinions on topics ranging from their education at Heritage Christian Academy to countries they would like to visit.

Maegan is beautiful, very expressive and practical. She is a delight to talk with on the phone. She reasons out everything. She's a careful shopper. I love listening as she practices her flute while we are on the phone together. Even while practicing, she wants to be perfect as she does each song.

Maegan on Grandparents" Day with Grandma and Grandpa Gibson and Grandpa Davey

Lovely Jessica looks for the needs of everyone else. When Maegan wanted a certain American Girl doll, Jessica would remind me every time we talked on the phone. When we gave the doll to Maegan for her birthday, Jessica was probably as happy as Maegan that she received the doll. Jessica also is a horse lover and takes riding lessons. I'm looking forward to being able to watch her ride in the near future.

"Joshua, Grandpa Davey has a secret, but you can't tell anyone."

Joshua is the strategist. He has been able to win at checkers since the first time he learned to play. He and I enjoy playing with our Lincoln Logs. We bought him two boxes, and I have two boxes here.

James and Maegan watch Joshua Gibson receive
his Lincoln Logs on Christmas

He's very creative. Like I was at his age, he's not too tall, and competitive in every sport he plays. I predict he will be an accountant or an executive when he grows up.

I'll never forget 1999 Christmas day. Susan and James' family were over for dinner and gift exchange. For some reason, seven-year-old Maegan, normally a contented child, was having a bad day. Susan had earlier told me that the children needed hats, gloves and scarves for dress and play. We selected two pairs for each of the girls and one set for Joshua. The sets with Cinderella and Snow White were for the girls to wear while playing out. The other set was velvet, and was for dress. When Maegan opened her first gift, it was the casual set. She put her hands on her hips and stated in a most disgusted fashion, "I have a hat and gloves. Why did you get me another pair?" Susan explained that her old set was too small for her. When Jessica opened hers, she turned around, smiling, and said, "Thank you Grandpa and Grandma." After opening other gifts, Maegan was given the velvet set. When she opened the package and recognized what they were, she exploded. "What is this, another hat and gloves? I don't need more hats and gloves!" She went on and on until James had her stand in the corner of the dining room by the coat closet. Jessica unwrapped hers and simply said, "Thank you Grandpa and Grandma. These are for church, aren't they?" We both agreed. The last gift Maegan opened was the 50 one-dollar-bills that I had wrapped in a box. Immediately she proclaimed, "I got one hundred dollars." I told her there wouldn't be that many. She insisted there would. Jessica opened hers and beamed, "Thank you Grandpa and Grandma Davey. This is a lot." She took them out of her box and fanned them. I took her picture, and James had her put them back into the box for safekeeping. In the meantime, Maegan moved over to the corner on the floor next to the door, and began counting her dollars. When she realized there were only 50 one-dollar bills, she really exploded, "What?! There's not one hundred dollars, there's only fifty dollars in here. Where is the rest of my one hundred dollars?"

On Christmas morning, Maegan ponders,
"Where's my other fifty dollars?"

Anne or I took a picture of her, but I had to go to our room and lean against the bed. I was laughing so hard I thought I would fall out of my chair. If I recall correctly, Maegan was soon back in the corner. She complained, mumbling during the entire time she was in the corner. I believe James put her there two or three more times because of her attitude. She continued to complain about the money or the hats. Joshua was a baby in arms and happy the entire day. The day convinced me that in the future, we need to take the children shopping for their gifts. I have never seen Maegan in a bad mood since that day.

Joshua Gibson driving Uncle Max's boat

How I look forward to more talks on the telephone, more tea parties, and the overnight visits from the grandchildren. They delight us.

JULIE AND DAVID

When I hired Anne, she told me about her children, Julie and David. Conditions of her accepting the position hinged on her being allowed to communicate with them when they arrived home from school, and that she would be allowed to attend their school activities. They met me before Anne would take the job, and I told them if they needed to talk to someone, they could call me. They often did. When David would call, he would ask me a question, or tell me one or two things, and hang up immediately with no goodbyes, a man of few words. I loved his calls.

Julie and David have always been advocates for people with handicaps. Once the wheelchair signs were used in parking lots, David always carried cards to put on cars without an authorized card or license plate. The card admonished people not to park there if they had no handicap.

Julie was extremely busy in high school. She was a great swimmer, a champion with the butterfly stroke, in plays, helped build floats, and at noon she hosted a half hour radio program. She also sang with a high school group from church. They traveled on weekends to sing in Michigan, Indiana, and Ohio. During her senior year she worked in a local medical office.

About six months before Anne and I got married, Julie decided to attend church with her boyfriend instead of with us. One Sunday the congregation held a meeting after church to discuss the addition the church was planning. Several of the members didn't want the expense involved to have a wheelchair entrance and elevator built since the church didn't have anyone attending who used a chair. Julie was quick to point out that there was no one attending in a wheelchair because they couldn't get up the many steps to the entranceway.

Julie was silent when they started talking about the baptistery. A member spoke up and said he had talked to David Davey at Goodwill regarding the cost. He said Mr. Davey was willing to call someone in Lansing to get the church a special exception for the baptistery. The member offered to ask Mr. Davey about the entranceway. Julie was quick to point out the difference in the two issues. After much discussion, the building chairman put the meeting on hold for a week.

Julie and her boyfriend were getting a ride home with the man who planned to call me. When they stopped at Julie's house, Anne, David and I were sitting in the front yard. Julie quickly introduced us. The man and I spoke for a few minutes. I told him I had called and obtained the permit for exception of the baptistery. When he mentioned the entranceway, I asked him if he was telling me I was never welcome to visit their church. He was quick to apologize for even considering an entryway that was not accessible. I recommended he use the accessible entranceway to advertise in the yellow pages. I encouraged him to market it as a way for their church to bring in new members. Julie quickly pointed out there were probably many people in their church who had bad legs who would welcome an entranceway with no steps. The man called me a few months after the addition was completed. He asked me to check it out, and asked me to tell Julie that they already had two new members in wheelchairs. Also, he said Julie had been right about some of their members welcoming an entranceway with no steps. Julie was in the Navy by that time, but felt exonerated of misunderstandings at her comments during the meeting.

We were amazed when Julie made a hovercraft for her senior year woodworking class. It was made from marine plywood, with a six-bladed airplane propeller. It was a monstrous project. Before she began that project, she had made a large puppet stage for puppet shows she and Anne performed at church.

After high school, Julie served as an air traffic controller in the US Navy for five years. She married shortly after she joined the Navy. When Julie served on Guam, she divorced her husband. It was there that she met Stacy, also an air traffic controller. They have been lifetime partners ever since.

Julie and Stacy in Vigo, Guam sitting next to Japanese memorial. They met on Guam where both were US Navy Air Traffic Controllers.

Julie and I talk on the phone often. I've always loved those talks. She shares her innermost thoughts and dreams. Julie likes to weigh her options. She called me at work regarding the best solutions to different concerns. She usually had considered all the pros and cons before she called. After talking with me for a few minutes about them, she nearly always would suggest that, after weighing her options, she could only see one solution, and her discernment of the situation was usually the wisest. If I have other thoughts, she will listen very carefully and take some time before making a decision.

Dave visiting with Stacy and Julie in Canada at the train station on their tour of Americas

Julie has always reminded me of Anne. Julie has proven she is a leader and capable of obtaining many high-paying positions if money was her priority. It hasn't been for many years. She needs to enjoy her work. Wherever she chooses to accept a new job, she will go in and organize the office and responsibilities. She just can't help it. When she was in retail, she ran the model store near Detroit, Michigan for her company. When she went to her first mall managers meeting, she was told that the woman who had been secretary had transferred to another store. One of the men told Julie that she would replace the woman as secretary, and started to hand Julie the pen and paper. Julie immediately let them know that she was not a member of the Good Ole Boys Club. The first male secretary served that day. Julie was still steaming when she called me at Goodwill to ask my opinion of her action. My reaction of course was, "Way to go!"

Julie has never liked injustice. When she was working in the model store at the mall, it was obvious the city where it was located wanted to keep all minorities out of their park. They posted signs that said you had to be a resident of that city to use the park. Since the city had never allowed any minorities to buy property in the city, it was evident it was unlawful. An employee of a local newspaper came to the local businesses to ask the managers of the mall their opinion of the law. Julie told them she smelled the KKK. The other managers said they didn't have an opinion. The next day the headlines read, "Local Store Manager Smells the KKK in the Park." The paper reported that Julie ate there and was never questioned about her residency. A Detroit TV station came to the store to see if Julie was willing to participate in a panel discussion regarding it. She declined. However, many of the Detroit churches told their parishioners to boycott all the other stores and shop only at Julie's store. She set new records for sales. The law was eventually banned. When she called me to share her decision, Julie thought her company might be angry. When the sales soared, they congratulated her.

David has always been a hard worker. He had a paper route when he was 12. He would deliver the weekend papers at midnight or whenever the Gazette delivered them to his corner. When the weather was nice, he and his friends delivered them on foot or on their bicycles. If the weather wasn't so good, Anne and I often drove him.

David played Little League baseball and Rocket football for several years. He was on the Portage Central High School football team for three years.

When David was sixteen, he unloaded trucks at Meijer Thrifty Acres. His supervisor promoted him to working leader on his second night. At Discount Tire, he changed tires outside in all kinds of weather. During college summer breaks, he sprayed lawns for Tru-Green. He was out in the morning when it was still dark, and worked until it was dark. All of his supervisors praised his excellent work attitude. When he was on a full scholarship at the University of Michigan in Ann Arbor, he scrubbed pots and pans for his spending money. Ambition and integrity have always been a part of David.

At church, David was always at the front door, greeting new students. He escorted the visitors to class and introduced them to other classmates and to us since we were the youth leaders.

We visited David when he was a freshman at University of Michigan in Ann Arbor. Anne and I were on our way into his dorm when Anne noticed almost all of the men in the dorm had on new earrings. Anne told me how glad she was that David didn't want to have his ears pierced. When we entered his room, there sat David with his new gold earring. I was proud of Anne as she complimented him on how great he looked in gold. He wore it home three or four times, but took it off before he joined his Christian friends. After two or three months, he put it away for good. In addition to his schooling at the University of Michigan, David has earned a Bachelor degree from the University of Texas in Austin, and two Masters.

*Mom Helen Simpson, Aunt Ella, Anna and John Eley at
David and Cindy Laramie wedding reception*

Two years later, David joined the US Navy. Shortly after his graduation from Basic Training, we enjoyed standing in line with David and his lovely bride, Cynthia, after they were married in the Warsaw, Indiana Church of God. He and Cynthia have two children, Lucy and Philip.

When he was stationed in Bremerton, Washington, David was scheduled to fly to San Diego to attend a Navy training session. He called to tell us that he had arrived safely. When we asked him about the flight, he was proud to tell us that he and Cynthia had decided that they could save money if he drove his motorcycle, instead of flying. We asked if it was safe to ride that far alone. His voice was happy when he told us that he wasn't alone. As soon as he pulled out of Bremerton, onto the highway, he found himself in the center of a large group of Hell's Angels, heading to San Diego. He rode among them, and said they were treated with great respect whenever they stopped for food or gas. He said they made excellent time. When we hung up from talking to him, we praised God for His protection of David and his hosts.

Cynthia and the children had to stay in the States while David was out to sea. When we were visiting the family in Connecticut, Anne was given a tour on the USS Providence submarine. David was the Supply Officer. The crew told Anne they really appreciated David making pancake breakfasts and pizza nights weekly for everyone.

Lucy was our first grandchild and has always been very special.

Lucy and Anne watch Dave as he is taking pictures of them

When she was quite young, she loved to fly alone to visit us. We would meet her as she got off the plane at O'Hare Airport in Chicago. We'd go to a nice hotel downtown and visit some of the museums or the aquarium before coming back to Portage, Michigan.

Lucy and Grandma Davey after Lucy had just baked her first cherry pie

Lucy was seven or eight when she baked her first cherry pie here, and took it back on the plane with her to Bremerton, Washington. Cynthia let her freeze it until David returned from a tour in the USS Michigan submarine.

Sometimes when Lucy was here, we went down to Essenhaus in Middlebury, Indiana Amish country to eat, shop, or for Lucy and Anne to go on the horse and buggy.

Even as a young child, Lucy was a very good skater. She loved our wide driveway. She could skate while pushing me in my wheelchair.

Lucy practicing some new tricks on her roller skates in our driveway

Lucy and I loved to go fishing. One day we came home with her great catch. When she showed the many fish to Maegan and Jessica, Jessica wanted to pet the fish, but Maegan, being practical, allowed Lucy and our son-in-law, James, to clean them so we could eat them. Lucy and I became best friends due to our talks while she pushed me around, or went fishing together.

Granddaughter Lucy looking at Niagara Falls during her first helicopter ride

Our neighbor, Don Campbell, was the official Santa Claus at some events in the community. He took a long time to dress and was a perfect Santa. On Christmas one year, he came back from giving gifts to children in his rental houses. He called Anne and asked if he could come over to bring the children some gifts he had. David was out pulling the children on the sled, and came in at that time. The children were just getting out of the bathtub when Santa knocked on the door. The children's eyes were big as saucers when they sat on his knees as they opened their gifts. Lucy was very serious as she told him, "Santa, I have never seen your reindeer so I'd like to get dressed and go see them." Santa explained he would have loved that but he had to go to several houses he hadn't visited yet.

Cousins Lucy Laramie with Maegan Gibson wearing her red tap shoes

Lucy has a great talent for playing the viola. Anne flew out to Connecticut to attend Lucy's concert when she was in junior high. Lucy's teacher told Anne that, with her talent and her excellent grades, Lucy could get a full scholarship to Harvard or any university in the United States if she was willing to play in the school's orchestra. Unfortunately, David was transferred to a naval base in San Diego; orchestra was not offered in the San Diego schools, so Lucy was unable to play on a regular basis. I hope she joins a local orchestra when she is out of college.

Lucy calls me every day since I am spending so much time in bed. She's a nanny during the day so we talk as she drives to school from work, or home at night. I love the stories she shares about the children she is helping to raise. I'm delighted when she calls and asks my advice on many areas. It's fun to be a grandpa.

Lucy Laramie and Grandma Davey 2004 Christmas picture

I'm sure Lucy will not stop attending college until she gets her doctorate in Psychology. I believe that someday Lucy will be the owner, president or executive director of a company or agency, such as Goodwill. She has the heart, ability and compassion needed for the job.

Philip reminds me so much of David when he was Philip's age. A few minutes after he arrives here, he comes into the house with half of the boys in the neighborhood. They have quickly become his friends so he shares popsicles, candy, or whatever we have purchased especially for him. He is tall, gentle and kind.

When Philip was three or four, David was out to sea. One evening I received a call from a very frustrated Cynthia. After hearing about her day, I told her I wanted to come out to Washington and give her a hug. Philip had awakened and taken his large Tonka truck into the pantry and was making a cake with five pounds of flour and sugar, among other things in the dump truck. That afternoon he came around the back of the house to announce that he had just filled up her gas tank. The water hose was still by the car. He always has been such a helpful young man. And smart! When he was in the fourth or fifth grade, Anne asked him what his favorite subject in school was. He told her spelling. His teacher assigned the class five or six words. They had to write the meaning of each, using each in four sentences, with each having one of the meanings. He told her you never forget the spelling when you do that. He told her the words. We didn't tell him, but we had to look them up in the dictionary because we had never heard of them, nor could we spell them. Philip has a great vocabulary.

One year Philip was here for a few weeks in the summer so he was able to attend the Christian Learning Centers at church. He took the fishing class. He caught several fish, but the one largemouth bass he caught was less than one eighth of an inch too short to keep. Most kids would have kept it anyway, but Philip said that would have been dishonest so he threw it back. His lesson on integrity impressed those in his class.

Anne got permission from Cynthia for Philip to fly in an open cockpit, World War I trainer biplane. The owner, Alan Wright, told Philip that he would let him fly the plane for five minutes, and gave Philip directions on what he should do. The runways were busy with commercial planes coming in so they were in the air for over an hour instead of the scheduled twenty-minute flight. When the plane landed, Philip thanked Mr. Wright, then was very serious when he told Anne, "Grandma, do you remember when Mr. Wright told me I could fly the plane for five minutes?" When Anne nodded, he said, "It's okay Grandma, because I really enjoyed flying the plane and he said I did a good job. I was watching the second hand on my watch and I only got to fly for four minutes and forty seconds, but that's okay." When Anne told me, I could just imagine David saying that when he was Philip's age of eleven.

Philip, just like David did as a boy, loves to visit the Army surplus stores that sell almost everything. He loves to buy patches and many other things. He also loves to go to the gun shop. I would expect he will go into the military for at least one tour after his college. Or maybe he will be a cop.

When he was still a small child, a large dog ran into Philip, knocking him down, and causing a severe brain injury. He was flown from Bremerton to Seattle, Washington where emergency surgery was performed. Cindy called us and everyone else she knew to ask our churches to pray for Philip. We had most of the churches in Kalamazoo, our relatives' and friends' churches in Europe, Florida, Indiana, Michigan, Ohio, and New York, praying for him. It was a miracle that he quickly was totally healed, and was home that week.

Anne's comments:

David retired in 2018 as a Commander in the Navy. Besides his six month tours at sea, David was stationed in Belgium, California, Connecticut, Florida, Georgia, Hawaii, Idaho, Indiana, Japan, Rhode Island, Saudi Arabia, Texas, and Washington.

Chapter 7

The Happiest Moment Of My Life

Dave wrote this chapter a few months before he died. His words began:

ONCE ANNE HAD said she would marry me, we planned a very small wedding. We sent out twenty-five invitations. Ken Shaw agreed to be my best man. Anne's son David agreed to be the usher. Anne's friend Grace Miller was Anne's matron of honor. David Golland was our photographer; our pastor, Dennis Young, married us on October 29, 1977. The only relatives able to attend, besides David, were my mom and dad, and Anne's brother Jim.

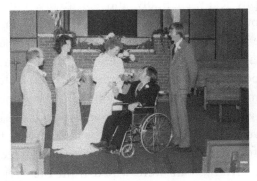

*Dennis Young, Grace Miller, Anne and David
Davey, Ken Shaw at our wedding*

Our wedding was so special. To me, Anne was the most beautiful bride in the world. We loved each other's vows, and everyone told us they had never seen a couple more in love than we were. The only things I remember are the vows and Anne's wonderful eyes. It was the happiest moment of my life when Dennis Young declared we were man and wife.

I rewrote my wedding vows many times in the weeks after Anne agreed to marry me. During our wedding, I was shaking so hard I could barely hold my notes. Anne's eyes never left mine as I spoke, "My darling Anne. You have awakened my ability to love unconditionally, knowing I can emphatically say I trust you to never purposely cause me any unhappiness, embarrassment, hurt feelings, or sorrow. I know that you want only the best for me.

"For years I had forgotten how to love, how to trust, how to respect my feelings. For many years, I felt like I could do no right, that I was less than normal, but you have shown me love and trust that gives me confidence to face the world. You are an encourager.

"You are the world's best mom. I know that if anything happens to me before Susan is grown, you will do all that is in your power to see that she will experience your unending love.

"I have never known anyone with your capacity to love and forgive. You are a great role model. I thank God that you love Him even more than you love the children and me.

"I promise I will love you forever, protecting you in every way that I can, physically, mentally and spiritually. I promise I will encourage you in any endeavor you choose, knowing you would never pursue anything that would not be best for our family. I promise you and God I will be the best dad to Julie and David that is humanly possible. If anything happens to you before David is grown, I promise to raise him in a loving Christian home. Julie and David will always have a home with me if they desire it.

"Thank you Anne for loving me. Thank you for agreeing to be my wife, for better or worse. I adore you. I pledge you my undying love." Many tears were wiped from the eyes of the men and women attending.

Ken Shaw, Grace Miller, Anne and Dave Davey, Bill and
Helen Simpson (Dave's parents) at our wedding

As Anne read her vows to me, I couldn't help but shed tears. I believe there were no dry eyes in the church. As she held my hands during both our vows, I was shaking quite badly. I don't remember ever shaking before except when I was cold.

Dave and Anne Davey leaving the church as Grace
and Melanie Miller are throwing rice

Anne helped me by gently rubbing my hands. Twice she touched my cheek ever so gently with a finger for just a second. She also helped by silently blowing me kisses and looking intently into my eyes. I was so grateful. Her voice was soothing and clear as she declared, "I love you so much David. Constantly, I give thanks to God for His gift of our love. I love you David because you love God the most in your life. You will see that Christ is the Head of our home. That's very important to me. I love you because you are my very best friend. I value that friendship. I promise to always be your friend, and never betray that friendship. You look for the best in everyone.

"You show respect to all persons. I promise I will always respect you. In your hands I feel strength, yet gentleness; in your arms I feel loved and protected; in your eyes I see kindness, compassion, gentleness, understanding and patience. I promise to return these to you, so that the Lord may help us to grow in His love.

"From your lips come words of comfort and understanding; you are a peacemaker; you are unselfish, thinking of others first. I promise I will not be jealous or selfish of your time when the Lord sends someone who needs to talk to you.

"In your love, I feel beautiful. You are a person I can always look up to. And, very important to me, I see your great love for the three children—someone they can confide in, someone they can talk to and share their joys and disappointments.

"I no longer dread growing old, but look forward to sharing those years with you, serving the Lord together and sharing and studying His Word with you. My Darling and my friend, before God and our friends, I pledge you my everlasting love. Please treat it gently.

OUR HONEYMOON

Because Susan was singing on TV Sunday morning, we decided to delay our honeymoon until Monday, October thirty-first.

For our honeymoon, we drove down to a motel near the entrance to Shenandoah Valley Drive. There was a dense fog for the last two hours before we finally saw the motel sign. We planned to take the Drive the next morning to go into Washington DC.

When we ordered our dinner, Anne was disgusted when the waitress came over to the table and asked her what we were having. Anne let her know that I was an executive, and kindly told the woman to never insult anyone in a wheelchair by not talking directly to him or her. The waitress apologized to me, and took our order. Anne repeated this advice for several years until the public finally seems to be educated.

As we ate in the motel restaurant, we overheard a conversation that sounded like the two men sitting in the booth behind us were planning something illegal, possibly involving a murder, and making it appear to be a Halloween prank. We felt like there was an evil cloud over them. We quickly went to our room. There was no phone, and we were both afraid. We didn't bring in our bags, but slept fully dressed, and left before it was light. It was definitely not the honeymoon we'd planned. The Drive was closed because of the dense fog, so I suggested we drive through Kentucky and go to St. Louis, Missouri.

We enjoyed the horse farms and animals as we drove through the Kentucky countryside. In 1977 there were no cell phones. During the entire trip, we used my CB to talk to truckers and other travelers. My handle was "Daddy McWheels." I told one truck driver we were newlyweds. Apparently many others heard me.

David and Anne Davey on their honeymoon in St. Louis

All the way to St. Louis, people on CB's were asking if the honeymooners were out there, and congratulating us on our marriage. I enjoyed talking to them. We loved every minute of our honeymoon in St. Louis. Everywhere we went was wheelchair accessible, including the Zoo, Gardens, and the Showboat on the Mississippi River. On the way home, we stopped to see Aunt Ella and Uncle Walter on the farm.

Dave and Anne visit with Aunt Ella and Uncle Walter.

THE MAKEOVER

In 1977, I was still wearing the brown shoes I wore in college. Since I didn't walk on them, the soles were like new. The hundreds of coats of polish they received in the twenty years, made the top of the shoes an unusual shade. They were no longer in style, plus I didn't have any slacks or suits that went with that shade of brown shoes. One day at work, before we were married, Anne gently let me know that my brown shoes didn't go with my blue or black suits. She told me that she wanted to buy me a good pair of Florsheim's for my birthday present. Since I was pretty conservative, Anne was surprised when I chose a pair of burgundy "short boots" that were popular in the 1970's. When I told the man at Florsheim's that I wore size eight and a half, Anne grimaced and asked him to please measure my feet. When the man announced I should be wearing size ten and a half, he looked at me and told me I was lucky I didn't have any corns or calluses. I had never mentioned it to Anne, but I told the shoe salesman that I had many corns and calluses on both feet. By the time we were married in two months, with the help of the Florsheim's, my feet had healed, and I threw away my box containing Dr. Scholl's patches.

When we were first married, Anne was alarmed when she saw raw scars on the left front area around my waist, caused by my back brace. I figured that sore area would always be there. I kept one or two folded handkerchiefs between my skin and the back brace. Anne was concerned about infections. She insisted they were there because I needed to have my back brace redesigned. In a very short time, after I was properly measured and two new braces were sewn by Mary Mulder, the scars nearly disappeared. There was no more bleeding.

Anne was very concerned when I told her about the ringing in my ears. When I admitted it had been years since I had seen a doctor, she attributed the ringing to high blood pressure. She insisted I go to her family doctor. Dr. Bloch said my blood pressure was great and I was extremely healthy. He watched me as I buttoned the top button on my shirt. He advised me that I needed a larger neck size on my shirts or I could have ringing in my ears. Anne measured me, and then bought me a new shirt wardrobe, replacing my fourteen and a half shirts with size sixteen and a half. I never had ringing in my ears again.

On our honeymoon, Anne was also alarmed when she noticed I had sore scars under both my arms. I told her my back brace and suits caused them. Apparently suits off the rack don't have enough room under the arms to allow for the friction caused from wheeling my chair. I told Anne that nearly all suits are made that way because most people don't have the extra flesh I had from the back brace pushing it up. When we returned from our honeymoon, we went into Hepp's in Kalamazoo. I explained my problem to Ben Brot. Anne asked Ben to find me some good suits with a little more underarm room. I nearly choked when I saw the price of good suits, but I was pleased with the difference in the comfort under my arms. They are definitely cut differently. When I tried on three different suits to determine which jacket was more comfortable, or which color I preferred, Anne smiled and said I looked great in all of them. She had Ben bring out two good sports jackets that could be worn with all my slacks. They felt terrific. Anne and Ben felt it would be foolish to only buy one and have me continue to wear suits and jackets that were keeping me raw under the arms. Ben told Anne that if she bought two suits and one jacket, he'd throw in the other two free, so Anne bought them all. She felt that I needed to get clothing that protected my skin. Anne was concerned that I could get skin cancer or a bad infection from open sores. After wearing those new suits for a few weeks, my scars were gone. Within a week, I donated all my old suits and jackets to Goodwill. When Ben went out of business, we had my suits tailor-made by Mike at M&W. What a difference those few changes made in my everyday comfort. After we were married a few months, I loved to tease Anne and tell her that I was no longer the man she married.

Chapter 8

They Said It Was Barrrier Free Ski Lodge

AFTER DAVE AND I were married, Michigan Association of Rehabilitation Facilities (MARF) began holding special seminars annually in the middle of ski season, at a popular ski lodge near the Leelanau Peninsula in Michigan. I always attended with Dave. The logistics of the wheelchair accessible room to the dining room and meeting room made it impossible for him to attend alone. Our room was wheelchair accessible. There were no small doorways, but it was not barrier free. When I moved our double bed three feet toward the window, there was plenty of room for Dave's wheelchair. It made it accessible, but certainly not comfortable, because the bedroom was always over one hundred degrees, except for about five feet on my side of the room.

Our bedroom window faced the heated swimming pool on the right. The steam from the pool was very hot and our room felt like we were in a hot cloud. Facing left, the bright lights that lit the ski slopes made it unnecessary for us to ever turn on the bedroom light at night. The ski slopes ended next to the swimming pool, just a few feet from the wall beneath our bedroom window. The skiers and swimmers were laughing and screaming under our window at all hours. The floor on my side of the bed was cold as ice and slippery from the window draft. The bed was quite cold for at least sixteen inches on my side, but we snuggled on Dave's side of the bed.

The bathroom was more like a sauna, with no exhaust fan. Dave complained the first year we used the room, but was told the lodge had central heat, and to feel free to keep the window open, which we did. Nothing cooled the bathroom.

The main dining room had two or three steps going up from MARF's meeting area, but no ramp. We were forced to go outside the room, using a door only a foot away from the dining room. I was able to tip Dave back and push him around the side of the building on a wooden walkway, through the kitchen, past the food staff, and into the dining room. Of course the wooden planks of the walkway were snowy and slippery so I had to replace my shoes with boots, and we both needed to wear a warm coat. We got acquainted with the kitchen help, but a twenty second walk up the few steps for everyone else took us two or three minutes, six times a day. Our comfort was dependent on how much new snow covered the icy wooden planks. Once seated, the food was wonderful. Their homemade cinnamon rolls were fabulous. The aroma wafting into our bedroom, while they baked, woke us each morning.

One day the meeting broke for lunch a half hour sooner than planned. I was shopping, and planned to meet Dave for lunch. An attendee of the MARF meeting offered to quickly push Dave to the dining room so he wouldn't have to don his coat. He obviously had never pushed a wheelchair on snow before. He didn't realize the wheelchair needed to be tipped up so it was on its big back wheels. When the men went outside on the wooden walkway, the small front wheels that turned on Dave's chair got caught on the boards many times. The man slipped and fell, and he nearly knocked Dave out of his wheelchair seat when his head hit the back of Dave's chair. Dave couldn't see the man since he was behind him, but the man acknowledged he was hurt. Without boots, he was slipping and sliding. It took them nearly ten minutes to go the short distance. The man, with his suit ripped and wet, was probably as embarrassed as he was frustrated when they finally arrived at the kitchen door, and I opened it. I was just heading out to find them. Both of them, dressed only in suits, were quite chilled. A man with bloody knees and hands, and ripped suit, certainly drew attention to the dangers of a snowy wooden walkway. Dave believed the incident was an eye opener for the attendees who served the handicapped but hadn't personally experienced incidents of concern over 'minor' obstacles. Dave and I felt we received much more respect after that meeting.

MARF'S HEADQUARTERS

When Michigan Association of Rehabilitation Facilities was planning their next meeting, Dave got a call from MARF's Executive Director, Chuck Foster. He was bragging about the newly renovated barrier free building in Lansing where the meeting would be held. Apparently Chuck was referring to Dave's experiences at the ski lodge and other locations when, "Your problems are over David," was his promise. He assured Dave there was no need for me to join him because the building, including the parking lot, was barrier free. The day went well and it was an hour past working hours when the meeting was finally ended. All the other attendees fled immediately. Dave stayed to talk with Chuck for a short time.

Dave decided to use the restroom next door before leaving for home. As he opened the door, another man was coming out and held the inside door open for Dave. Once inside, Dave remembered thinking what a great barrier free restroom it was. He especially appreciated the privacy the second door gave because so many restroom doors open to the hall, and expose everyone at the urinal. As he started to leave, he was grateful for how easily the inside door swung out, but was unhappy when it closed behind him and he discovered the knob on the outer door was too high to open it. Dave soon realized it wouldn't have done him any good anyway, because the outside door swung in. There were only a few inches on either side so he couldn't turn his wheel chair around. He was stuck in the dead space between the doors. Of course this doorway design was not built according to code.

That was not a good place to be on a Friday evening after all the State employees were gone. God heard Dave's desperate plea. Fortunately, after Chuck realized Dave had been gone for a long time, and hadn't taken his coat and briefcase, he came to the door and managed to squeeze his head in to view Dave's predicament. A building maintenance employee was called, and he released Dave from his prison by removing the door's hinges. As the employee lifted the door away, everyone gave a sigh of relief. Dave was grateful the space between the bathroom and hallway doors didn't turn out to be a weekend retreat.

A MAJOR GROCERY CHAIN BECAME BARRIER FREE

Fred Meijer, the owner of a major grocery chain, called Dave in the 1960's, and asked for his input on how the owner could make his stores more wheelchair accessible. They talked about every aspect, including dressing room and restroom requirements.

When they discussed checkout lanes, Dave suggested that it was unnecessary for the store to design all of the checkouts wide enough for a chair. One or two wider checkout lanes, with a wheelchair sign above them, could be designated as wheelchair lanes, and allowing regular shoppers with a maximum of six to twelve items, to use the lanes if no wheelchair user was in sight. The owner used Dave's suggestions, and his stores were probably the first and best accessible of all the stores in Michigan.

One evening, years later, Dave and I were in a Meijer store, shopping for groceries after work. Dave was pushing the grocery cart, as I pushed his wheelchair. We had the cart piled high. Only one wheelchair checkout lane was open. The young man at the register spotted us as he was ringing up the few items from the cart in front of us. He rudely yelled to tell us we couldn't come through that lane because it was for people with only ten items or less. I pointed to the wheelchair sign, but he screamed loud enough that several cashiers down the row of cash registers heard him. They all pointed to the wheelchair sign. He was still belligerent as he announced he wasn't going to check us out, so to move to another register. In those years, none of the aisles of other registers was wide enough to accommodate a wheelchair.

I spotted the assistant to the Store Director. We knew her very well because Roger Kik, the store director, was on the Goodwill Board of Directors. Roger's assistant waved at us, and I signaled for her to come over. She was standing a few feet away from the checkout when the young man finished giving change to the customer ahead of us.

Once more he rudely told us he wasn't going to check us out, so we could just go somewhere else. I proceeded to unload our groceries. He was trying to get the next customer to bypass us. The other cashiers were furious at his rudeness. Customers were becoming irritated at him. The couple behind us, with a few groceries, tried to pass us.

Fire flew! The director's assistant was very angry by that time. Knowing the cashier had been properly trained and instructed that the lanes with a wheelchair sign are primarily for people using wheelchairs, she embarrassed him and the other couple as she apologized to us. She instructed the rude employee that anyone in a wheelchair has priority in those lanes, over anyone else, no matter how few groceries others have. Lanes without a wheelchair sign and stating, "10 Items or Less" are for all customers with few groceries. About forty or fifty people, who had overheard his rudeness, gave the director's assistant a round of applause. The couple behind us apologized for having tried to pass us. I thought I might have embarrassed Dave, but he said he was never more proud of anyone than he was of me that night. He felt I prevented many timid wheelchair users from being embarrassed in the future.

Chapter 9

Goodwill School Changes Lives

In Michigan, the public school system was required to provide schooling to students until they graduated or reached the age of twenty-five. Dave was a member of a committee who was given the responsibility to find a solution to dealing with students who were trouble makers or part of a dysfunctional family, but whose families wanted them to remain in the school system. Dave and another committee member told me that the planning meeting had gone on for nearly two hours with no suggestions for solutions. It was apparent to Dave that none of the members were thinking of win-win solutions for the kids, but all of the suggestions were for keeping the teachers happy when they had to deal with those students. Finally, the committee chairperson turned to Dave and asked for his input. Dave acknowledged that he was disappointed because not one person had suggested anything that was good for the children being served. Nearly every member was defensive and told Dave it was impossible to help these students, but the school system was forced to accept them. Dave's statement was that if they were alive, they could be helped. He told the committee if Goodwill was given the same amount of money per student that the public schools were given, Goodwill could help almost all of them. After much discussion, Dave told them if Goodwill could have fourteen children in the first year, eight of them would be successful. Although no one thought it was possible, they agreed to let Goodwill try. If four of the children even stayed in the program for the school year, the school system would consider it a success, Dave was told. Dave was quick to disagree, but he had a very short time to put together the staff needed for such an experiment. The staff was carefully selected and trained to deal with the many obstacles that the committee warned Dave to expect. We were told that most of these students didn't want to learn, probably smelled, hadn't had a bath in months, never washed their hair, used profane language all the time, and showed no respect to anyone or anything.

On the first day of their arrival by bus, the students walked into the building, with plans to prove the program couldn't help them. They looked and smelled worse than we had thought. The fourteen students met in the cafeteria with Goodwill's administrative staff, Level Two supervisors, and staff specially trained for this project. They were served refreshments while Dave proceeded to tell them that every one of the Goodwill staff was there to help them succeed. He told them that he felt certain that several of them would be using loud, profane, and unacceptable language for awhile. When he explained he knew it wouldn't be for long because that is what people do when they are unsure of themselves and can't express what they would like to say, a shocked expression came across the faces of those students who planned to do so.

Each student was given food vouchers every day so they could eat three meals and two snacks in the cafeteria. At first, many of the staff lunches disappeared from the refrigerators. This was quickly resolved as the students learned to trust their teachers, respect themselves, and began to police the area.

The program paid the students a small stipend to teach them the use of money, as well as teaching them to take pride in the small tasks they were allowed to do. The work was always redone by the employee assigned to the job.

One of the students (I will call him John Doe) vacuumed the area in front of my desk every morning. He actually did a terrible job. Each morning as I cheerfully told him, "Good morning John," he would declare there was nothing good about it, swear, use several words I had never heard before, and kick my metal desk. It soon had an ugly dent in it.

I asked Dave for permission to eat lunch with this young man. Dave told me that he didn't have the authority to give me permission, but I needed to obtain it from his program manager. I was given permission on the condition that I was not to buy him anything; couldn't cook or bake him anything; I was not to take him to church or anywhere in my car; and that I was not to be rude to him under any circumstances. We weren't allowed to do anything for these students that a public school teacher couldn't do. John smelled so bad that the other students made him sit several tables apart from them. On the first day I sat down with him, he was quick to demand to know why I wanted to sit with him. I told him I wanted to get to know him better. He accused me of planning to call his school and tell them anything he said or did wrong. When I explained that none of the staff would be reporting anything to the school, but that I wanted to get to know the young man behind his façade. He asked what facade meant. I explained that everyone wears a mask to cover up their feelings, especially when they don't feel good about themselves. I told him that sometimes I didn't feel good, but no one knew because I smiled and that was my façade, my mask. He was angry as he told me, "I'm not wearing a mask; this ugly face is mine." I was sincere when I looked him straight in the face and told him he really had a very nice face.

I shared many things with him about my three children who attended Portage Central High School. Every day he seemed to trust me more.

One day he confided in me that his mother was an alcoholic and had a different man in their house every time she collected the welfare check for the kids. He lifted up his pant leg and showed me a horrible scar. He explained that once when a man was hurting his mother, he had tried to stop him. The man kicked his leg, removing most of the flesh until his bone was showing. His mother hit the man with a ball bat and he left. However, John's mother was afraid to take him to the hospital or to a doctor. She felt her three children would be taken from her and she would have no income. She cleaned the wound every day and put salve on it until it healed.

The house she rented was cold and the bathroom water didn't work in the sink or tub. They only had cold water in the kitchen. I explained that was illegal. He said his mom told him not to complain or they would be kicked out of the house. I was horrified when I learned who their landlord was. I told John that a friend of mine at church was the inspector of rentals for the City of Kalamazoo, and I would tell her of their situation without mentioning their name. That Wednesday evening, I shared his story with my friend. She told me she would pull a routine inspection on all of the rentals belonging to that landlord and would do John's house third or fourth so no one would give a thought as to anyone there reporting the offenses.

That Friday when he was given his first small stipend check, he nearly threw it on my plate when he demanded to know what that was all about. I explained what it was. He asked if he had to give it to his mother. Of course I explained that it was his to do with as he wanted. I told him he didn't have to tell anyone about it. He could cash it and use it for anything. I pointed to his identification badge and told him he could use it with the badge to get a twenty percent discount on purchases in the Goodwill stores. He was serious when he asked if he would be allowed to buy things for his brother and sister. I assured him he could. I had to smile when he demanded, "Anne, look at me! Do you think any bank teller in their right mind would cash this check for me?" As I looked at his dirty face, stinky dirty clothes and long, tangled hair, I told him I had to agree with him. I told him to have our accountant take it to the bank when he was taking Goodwill's deposit; he would cash it and make sure John had the money.

On Monday, I was at my desk when a nice looking, clean-cut young man asked how I was. He laughed and thought it was funny that I didn't recognize him. He had gotten clothes at Goodwill, cleaned up, and gotten a haircut. He no longer smelled. John came up and gave me a hug. He said that his house now had hot and cold water upstairs and down; they had heat; and the broken windows were replaced. He said his family was elated.

He told me about a talk he had with his brother and sister. They were surprised when he told them that the reason nobody liked them was probably their fault because they treated people like he used to. He shared his fears with me about his twelve-year-old sister who was starting to develop, and being noticed by men his mother brought home from the bar. We agreed his sister should lock herself in her room and not come out when a man was going to be with their mother. I told John that he and his siblings would benefit if they decided to attend the church that was in the same block as their house.

We talked about a friend of mine who attended that church with her family. I suggested that he and his siblings introduce themselves to her and her husband. They would probably help him and his family, as well as introduce them to other members. We agreed it would help them to have permission to call someone reliable if there was an emergency during the night. He used his next stipend to buy clothes for his brother and sister. A few weeks later, he told me they had attended the church and gotten to know several people who invited them over for dinner. My friend let John know that she and her husband would help them if they had problems.

John soon finished the Goodwill School program and received his high school diploma. We went to his graduation and met his family. His mother was visibly proud of John, and thanked the Goodwill staff for all they had done for her family.

Unfortunately, some of the other students had some difficulties. One girl was six months pregnant midway in the program, and because of uremic poisoning, was ordered to bed for the remainder of her pregnancy. She came to Dave and told him she was so sorry that she had not respected her body, and she really wanted to finish the program. He assured her that she could come back the following year. If the school or another program didn't sponsor her, Goodwill would. She had the baby and returned the following year. The last time she called Dave, she had gone to Kalamazoo Valley Community College at Goodwill's program's expense and was working for an attorney and supporting her baby. I believe that one young man was killed in a fight. I don't remember the details. One young man was arrested and had to go to prison. Dave went to court with him and pleaded for the judge to let him finish the program because he was a changed person, but the judge refused. Only one person actually quit the program. Goodwill was awarded additional contracts for the program during the following years. Kalamazoo Loy Norrix High School later started a large program entitled, "Extended Family," I believe. A friend of ours, Jack Dunn, an ordained minister, was one of the program managers that students reported to each morning. They were sharing their concerns with each other, and their grades and self respect improved continually. Another program to help the youth was run by John Campbell, a friend of ours. Both programs sought advice from Goodwill's special team.

At the Grape Festival in downtown Kalamazoo Bronson Park in the 1990's, Dave and I saw a very nice looking young man with his wife and two children. He stopped Dave and me, called us by name, and asked if we remembered him. We asked if he had been in our youth group at church. He laughed, shook his head no, and asked if we remembered the high school program we had at Goodwill many years before to help the youth from dysfunctional families. Of course we did. Dave told him that Goodwill was still running the program. The man told his wife the program was designed to help turn around troubled teenagers so they could finish school. He reminded us that he had kicked my desk every day for the first few weeks until he recognized the value of the program. Dave and I yelled, "John! You look great." He told his wife and us how Goodwill had helped him. Before he completed the program at Goodwill, the Goodwill staff recommended that he attend Kalamazoo Valley Community College (KVCC) on the joint project between Goodwill and KVCC. He said he did well, and went on to graduate from Western Michigan University. He told us that he had gotten a small apartment and had his sister and brother move in with him. Both his brother and sister attended KVCC through Goodwill, and were doing well. At the time we saw him at the Grape Festival, he told us of the excellent position he held with an outstanding employer since he graduated from WMU. He was a Deacon in the local church they attended. We were so proud of him and his accomplishments.

Dave and I were very touched when he put his hand on Dave's shoulder, looked at both of us, and tearfully told his wife, "Do you remember my telling you about the two people who saved my life?" She nodded, and he continued, "Well, these are those two people." Their two children watched the four of us adults crying as he and his wife hugged us.

Chapter 10

Hawaii—The Beautiful

THE 1978 GOODWILL Conference of Executives meeting was held in Honolulu, Hawaii. The Goodwill in Kalamazoo, Michigan didn't have the money for Dave to attend, so we paid for his expenses and for David, Susan and me to accompany him. We had foregone coming to this beautiful state on our honeymoon so we could share the time with the children. Dave and I had only been married nine months. Susan and David were friends; we hoped this trip would further bond their brother-sister relationship.

For the last half hour of the flight into Oahu, the beautiful blue water mesmerized us. Sailboats, motorboats, ships, and surfers filled the scene. As we were landing on the runway, the glistening water looked inviting. It seemed we would run out of runway before the plane came to a halt at the Honolulu Airport. Upon our arrival, Dave was lowered on a portable freight elevator; the children and I walked down the plane stairs to his side. Beautiful natives greeted us on the ground. They draped us with lovely flower leis that had the most wonderful scent; a soft kiss on each cheek came with the flowers. As we looked around, everyone had a smile on his or her face; this is paradise! This is Hawaii!

We planned this trip as our second honeymoon; we had reserved two adjoining rooms. When we checked in, adjoining rooms were not available, so we were given two rooms with twin beds. Our second honeymoon was put on hold as Dave and David shared one room; Sue and I shared the other. The rooms were clean, but smaller than we had envisioned for a four-star hotel. As is true in so many hotels, the bedroom and bath Dave used was barrier free, but the carpet in the rooms and hallways was plush. In most hotels, the accessible rooms are next to the elevator. We have often been awakened at all hours by the elevator's traffic, but not at this lovely hotel. It would have been difficult for Dave to get to the elevator alone. It seemed to be a city block away from the rooms. The chair was hard to maneuver on the carpet, even with someone pushing.

On the flight to Hawaii, David read "Jaws II". It was a popular novel at the time. Certain exciting portions he read from the book got our attention. Upon our arrival, we checked with Big Joe, the man who rented surfboards for the hotel located on Waikiki Beach. He assured us that guests were notified whenever sharks were spotted.

Dave's day began and ended with Goodwill breakfast and dinner meetings, leaving him no time to see the famous Waikiki Beach outside our walls during sunshine hours. The children and I spent most of our time at the hotel beach or in the pool. David learned to surf very well. We bought Susan an inflatable beach mattress that she lay on in the water and, using her arms, she kept up with David on his rented surfboard.

During the breaks between meetings, Dave had the opportunity to talk to the Goodwill CEOs. He used the time to share many of the programs he and Ken Shaw were pursuing. The CEOs were eager to hear more. Many of them later came to Kalamazoo to visit Dave as a result of their conversations.

After the meetings ended, we had a sixteen-day vacation. We visited Pearl Harbor and saw the sunken USS Arizona. Because Dave was in a wheelchair, we didn't have to stand in line for the two or three hour expected wait. The barrier free entrance let us on the boat to the memorial immediately. We were in awe to have the opportunity to see this famous memorial, left untouched by our government to remind us of all the ships that were sunk by the Japanese bombs on December 7, 1941. The feeling in the pit of my stomach as I walked on the platform above the sunken ship, is hard to describe. I have a lump in my throat thinking about it now.

The next day was spent at the Polynesian Culture Center. What an experience! The Center is owned and operated by the Mormon Church with most, if not all, employees being students at the local Brigham Young University. Dave took pictures of Sue's and my wearing grass skirts over our shorts. I took pictures of David and Sue climbing the palm trees. We tried food native to different Polynesian islands, watched the beautiful floats as they came down the river, and were told the cultural differences of neighboring islands.

In the evening we attended the spectacular grand finale show, which is the pride of the Center. Dancers had ancestors of many different cultures who perfected the dances years ago. During half time, we snacked on pineapple halves, filled with ice cream and native fruit. That was the opening night of a brand new show, so the theater was filled with employees of all local media. Because of Dave's wheelchair, we were given great seats. We were surprised to recognize Don Ho and many other celebrities sitting in our row. Also, we talked to some guests who came because they had received invitations on the mainland to see the new show opening. The costumes, using many feathers, were professionally done in many colors. After having walked miles to view sidewalk displays, and sitting through that fantastic show, we were exhausted on our return trip to the hotel.

The hotels have wonderful paved walkways to their portion of the beach, as well as to the restaurants and shops nearby. Dave and I took many romantic moonlit walks. The sound of the ocean was wonderful. It seemed like a dream come true…in Hawaii, with my love, my Dave.

There was so much to see on Oahu. We enjoyed eating breakfast and lunch in the small outside dining area. Birds came and sat on the corner of our table, waiting patiently for the leftovers. The meals were huge and so reasonable. There was a McDonald's across from the hotel. The children often ate there. To please the thousands of Japanese tourists that visit the islands, McDonald's sold as many Oriental dishes as they did traditional hamburgers and fries.

There were many camera crews doing filming throughout the islands. A favorite pastime for many Goodwill families was to watch the original TV show, "Hawaii 5-0" being taped. We had to detour when the nearby Holiday Inn driveway was being filmed for the show.

One day Dave and I went for a long ride through the countryside. Sue and David wanted to stay at the hotel and swim in the ocean. The plan was for the kids to sign for their meals, surfboard rental, etc., then when we came back, we'd shower and dress to have dinner at a nice restaurant. Dave had me drive down city and country streets that resembled our alleyways. We talked to many of the local people as we saw them out in their gardens; many could only speak Japanese. It was amazing how small some of the gardens were, but we were told they contained a family's food supply. Just before the national cemetery closed, we were out taking in the glorious view when the guard told us the gate was being locked. We quickly exited to return to the hotel.

After being gone nearly all day, we parked and took the elevator to our room. As one couple got out of the elevator on the fourth floor, they looked at us and said in a sympathetic tone, "Oh, you're the parents of those two kids on the beach today, aren't you?" With that, the elevator door closed behind them, leaving us alone. We didn't get a chance to ask anything before we were whisked away. It's amazing how many prayers you can say between floors. It was with great fear and trepidation that we unlocked the door to Sue and my room. No children! We had tears in our eyes as we hurried to the room next door. The kids were there with friends, enjoying a movie they had rented. "Thank you God!" we both shouted.

With both kids talking so fast, we could hardly understand the explanation of their afternoon experience. They were surfing quite a distance offshore when Sue noticed the crowd on the beach was yelling and motioning for them to come out of the water. As soon as she had told David, they noticed the fins swimming around them. David said the speed their arms generated was second to none; even a roadrunner would look like he was standing still next to them. They were up on the sand before they stopped. It turned out they had been circled by manta rays, not sharks, but Susan and David assured us that, to them, fins are fins.

After that, the kids used the pool. The only time they swam in ocean water again was on the island of Hawaii where there was an ocean pool, protected from sharks by coral and volcanic rock. We were sorry the kids had the bad experience, but after that, we enjoyed their company when we went sightseeing.

When we arrived at the hotel, we were told that the Shah of Iran, who was in exile with his family and employees, was staying in our hotel. We never recognized the Shah, his wife, nor any of their children, having any fun, or even leaving their suites, during our week in that hotel. On the second day we were there, we were told that his son was interested in a beautiful girl in the hotel. Later that day we discovered the beautiful girl was the daughter of a friend of Dave's. She was invited to dinner with the Shah's family, but refused. During their time at the hotel, the son's bodyguard tried to get permission several times for the son to date her. The parents told him she wasn't old enough to be dating anyone. On the last full day we were there, I went to the laundry room at the end of the hall to wash our clothes. When I came out of the laundry room, one of the bodyguards asked me what I was doing at that end of the hall. When I told him I was washing clothes, he told me that I was never allowed to use the elevator across the hall. That elevator belonged to the Shah. I assured him that we were leaving the next morning to fly to Maui. On the following morning, as the bellhop was taking our luggage to the central elevator, we looked down the hall to our left, and there stood the bodyguards. We couldn't help but realize the sad truth, that famous people in exile were really prisoners for their own protection.

We loved Maui, and considered buying a condominium there. We stayed in a lovely condominium at Kaanapali Shores. There were pools and a gazebo in the yard. Early each morning, we strolled to the gazebo where others sat around sipping free coffee. Many tourists were busy making leis from the flowers on the ground.

By the time we were relaxing on Maui, we had tired of eating in fancy restaurants. We were homesick for a salad and steak. We went shopping at a large grocery store. Dave and I couldn't stand the poi we had been served, so we were surprised by a two-year-old boy and his mother who were shopping next to us. The little boy was pointing to a bag of what we thought was white mush. He went bonkers as he kept shouting, "Poi, Mom, poi, can we have poi?" Dave and I figured his mother must have had a secret recipe. It had to be different than what we had tried at two restaurants. We bought salad makings and T-bone steaks, and Dave cooked them on the grill by the gazebo. There was a soft warm rain as he turned the steaks. Although the rain hit us, it dried before we became wet.

The next day we went to the small store on the grounds. There was one small jar containing three or four ounces of peanut butter for $3.55. We bought that and a loaf of bread. We each ate a peanut butter sandwich that tasted like a little bit of heaven. The next morning Susan finished scraping the jar for her toast. David took a piece of bread and literally wiped the jar clean as he devoured the last hint of peanut butter. It's funny what you miss when you're away from home.

We loved the sound of the water splashing against the shore as we slept with the sliding door open. I believe it was on Maui that we came across a large breaker wall that appeared to have a million crabs clinging to it. Dave got a wonderful shot of the water splashing up and the crabs clinging to the wall. As the splash subsided, the crabs would scurry back and forth.

One day we planned to drive to the top of a mountain. In the winter, many tourists go there to ski. There was a typhoon coming toward the islands, and the wind was very strong. Susan and I are both afraid of heights, but, because the car was not equipped with hand controls, I was the only one who could drive. Dave and David were sitting on the right side of the car. By the time we were a quarter of the way up the steep and narrow mountain road, Sue and I were ready to go back down. However, the lack of anyplace to turn around forced me to continue. David sounded sincere as he'd comment, "Wow! Look at that drop between the palm trees here. I'll bet this car could turn thirty or forty complete somersaults before we'd land in the ocean. What do you think, Dad? Just look Mom and Sue!" By that time, Susan was on the floor of the back seat. About half way up the mountain, I saw a turn-around area, and we quickly descended to flatter ground.

It was hard for Dave and me to remember which of the islands are known for what landmarks. Each is so unique in its own right. After Maui, Kauai seemed remote and very undeveloped. As soon as we drove the station wagon out of the airport, we decided we had to have something to eat. The Golden Arches of McDonald's beckoned to us. Dave sat in the car to wait for the three of us to carry out the food. As David opened Dave's door, before he could hand Dave the food, hundreds of huge roaches appeared from under the seats and out of the walls of the station wagon. David backed away with dinner. Susan took the wheelchair around for Dave, and we quickly retreated to an outside table.

No sooner had we eaten than we returned the station wagon. When I went inside, they informed me they had no other vehicles that Dave could use. They asked us to get out, then they ran the vehicle through a spray to kill the insects; it looked like a carwash, but smelled like insect spray, inside and out. They gave us a spray can of insect poison they said was very strong. They suggested we might want to spray the apartment before we brought in any food. We never saw roaches again.

At one sight, there was a rushing river between two mountain peaks. Quite high above the rushing waters was a cement bridge, connecting the two mountains. It took all of my courage to push Dave out onto the bridge. Before we made it across to the other side, both of us felt weak at the knees. It was the first time we had the courage to venture that high.

As we were stopping at a small roadside tourist shopping area, we became alarmed when we thought the island was on fire. Huge fields around us were all ablaze, with smoke rising from the flames. The natives laughed and told us that sugar cane is set on fire to seal in the sugar before the cane is taken to the sugar factories. Later that evening we saw huge truckloads of the sealed sugarcane on its way to the factory.

What a lovely day going to the Fern Grotto was; we almost felt the presence of eyes watching from the jungle, as the boat glided down the river. The band was making beautiful music for us to sing along as we enjoyed the view. As we heard the history of this island, I could imagine how dangerous this ride would have been two hundred years ago. We were delighted to see that the Fern Grotto had a paved walkway that made pushing Dave's wheelchair easy. Many people were standing and whispering inside the natural amphitheater. We were fifty or sixty feet away from them, and could clearly hear their conversation. The ferns seemed to grow out of the very stones, from the ground, from the sheer walls of rock, and from the rocks hanging overhead. It was truly impressive.

BARRIER FREE RUNWAY? NOT!

We were flying from the Kauai airport to the large island of Hawaii, our final Hawaiian destination. We would be flying to Chicago from that airport in a week. As we got to the Kauai airport, the wind was picking up from the typhoon that would be hitting the island within the next twelve days. We were told that the staff would first load an older woman who used a wheelchair, then Dave, onto the old 737 jet that flew between islands. As we waited for the lady to be brought out, the chair lift was put into place; a family member pushed the woman onto the runway near us, kissed her goodbye, and left her alone. The brakes had not been locked before he left her, and the woman apparently had no ability to manage her own chair. A second or two later, a strong wind whipped past Dave. His brakes were intact while David and I still held onto the back of Dave's chair as tightly as we could. A second gust of wind directed the older woman and her chair down the long runway. All available employees and fast runners were in hot pursuit, as the chair continued faster and faster until it was out of our sight. The runway had to be totally smooth, without a stone or crack, or her chair would have turned over.

While awaiting her fate, they loaded Dave and the remaining passengers. The flight was postponed nearly half an hour before the woman was safely pushed back to the airport. She made the decision that she was not emotionally able to fly at that time. The flight proceeded to Hawaii.

On the lovely isle of Hawaii, we were scheduled to stay four nights at the Kona Hilton and three nights at a smaller hotel on the other side of the island in Hilo. As we drove from the airport, we passed many small hotels, surrounded by tiny shops and restaurants, all overlooking the marinas and docks. To the right, we saw fishermen proudly being photographed with their huge 'Catch of the Day'. We later learned that most fishermen have pictures taken with their catch. The fish is then weighed and given to the boat owner. He or she sells them to the local cannery to be made into cat food.

We thought we had several miles to go to the hotel. The winding road began its curve to the right. As the curve of the road followed the ocean, we spotted what looked like a huge apartment building, with large balconies overlooking the ocean. Boxes of colorful flowering plants seemed to have ivy cascading over the sides, making the wall resemble a 3-D patchwork quilt. Susan declared we should stay there. David wholeheartedly seconded the motion. As the road straightened, we saw the sign "Kona Hilton" on the lawn of the lovely hotel. A loud, "Yippee" went throughout the car.

When we went into the Kona Hilton, the manager greeted us warmly and told us our small Mountain View room would not be large enough to house the four of us. They hadn't been told we had two teenagers, so, for the same price, they gave us a corner suite, with both sides of the balcony overlooking the ocean. We thought we must be dreaming. The two king size beds in one room were accompanied by a king size hide-a-bed in the large living room. There was a small kitchenette next to the bathroom. This suite was definitely barrier-free. Immediately it was unanimous that all four of us preferred staying at the Kona Hilton instead of going over to Hilo for three nights. Fifteen minutes later, Dave had the hotel's approval for us to stay for the seven nights.

In some areas, the big island reminded us a lot of Michigan. At the time we were there, the Parker Ranch was considered the largest ranch in the world. As we drove there for lunch one day, the cowboys were riding on horseback over the thousands of acres they called home. We drove down the highway and stopped at the black sand and the green sand beaches. We saw bananas ripening on the trees at the side of the road. Many drivers stopped to sample them.

To go to Hilo, we had to go miles out of our way because the volcano had erupted five or six years before, spilling hot lava across the highway. We were told the inside of the hardened lava flow was still hot enough to melt land-moving equipment that, hopefully, would rebuild the road in the future. It was interesting to see ferns growing from the solid hardened lava. As we went up to have dinner at the Volcano Restaurant, the new growth of plants increased. I joined the many tourists who walked out onto the volcano. It looked like the roaring fire under the thick, hardened lava was very close to the wide crack I stood beside. There were many cracks with steam pouring out of them. Dave tried to rent a helicopter to take us over many of the sites so we could get a different perspective of it, but the helicopters had all been stored because of the coming typhoon.

Shortly after we returned home, the entire volcano blew its top and took the restaurant with it. Some of the small towns in our photos have since been totally burned by lava flows.

The sulfur fields were most interesting, but smelled terrible. We'd find steam vents from raised dry lava beds everywhere on the island. David got a wonderful picture of a huge spider on its web with a steam vent behind it. He was so close you could see the spider's eyes.

The view from our balcony was wonderful. We could watch kites sailing, with skiers holding onto the large sails. They were pulled speedily behind the ski boats until they were up sailing above the boats. The boats seemed to guide them as they maneuvered the towrope. What fun they seemed to have.

Other scenes were not so peaceful. All the tourists in the suites around ours were there with an organized tour group; they would come in exhausted from an all-day schedule and were told they had twenty minutes to meet at the doorway. We were so thankful that our time was unscheduled. We planned it a day at a time, but often changed our minds when we saw something more interesting.

One evening we felt especially grateful, while we looked at the ocean, that we had not taken a dinner boat. We watched swells build up at such a pace that all the professional surfers left their surfboards on shore and abandoned the whitecaps for the evening. The boats on the water were bouncing around so much that the waves hid them from our view each time the swells surfaced. We watched the three dinner boats as they went out into the ocean. These boats, surrounded by lights and decorated for the tourists, were recycled landing crafts remaining from World War II. Of course we could only see them half the time because the flat-bottomed boats seemed to ride a wave, and then disappear into it, time after time. Only a flicker of lights testified to the boats' existence as the voluminous waves foretold the winds that would whip this island in about ten days. Late that evening, tourists met us in the hallway. They looked dizzy or sick. They told us they wished they had gone to dinner with us when we invited them because they were on one of those flat bottomed boats. Their ride was worse than we had imagined.

Dave and I would often cross the courtyard on our early morning strolls. One thing we noticed was the luau area. We often watched as the employees prepared the hog for cooking. We talked to people who had gone to the luau. They explained the hog had already been cut up before the crowd arrived. The paid guests were each given about six ounces of roast pork, poi, a shish kebab of fruit and vegetables, and one drink. Other local snacks were on the tables. Singers and hula dancers entertained. Four or five natives mingled and talked to them. We didn't attend a luau. We chose to talk to natives in their yards or places of employment.

Early one morning, David awoke while the morning sun was still hiding beyond the horizon. He was delighted to be awake so early. He asked Dave if he'd like to take a stroll. They quickly dressed, and quietly left the suite. They strolled side by side down the meandering path lit by colored lights. They stopped to smell the brightly colored flowers that so generously bordered the walkway. It was a special time for a father and son to share. They thought they were the only two guests awake; all the other rooms were dark. Dave said they were sometimes silent, but they often laughed at something that might not have seemed funny if there was a crowd around. It was such a precious moment for both of them.

When Dave's arms and shoulders started to tire, they found a bench for David to sit down. Dave said they had fun reminiscing about all their adventures. Time seemed to go so fast. When they looked up, they realized they had talked longer than it seemed. The sun had risen, and they could hear guests talking in their rooms. Without saying anything, David grabbed hold of the handles in back of Dave's wheelchair and pushed him as they concluded their stroll.

DAVID MADE A NEW FRIEND

After breakfast, Dave, David, Susan, and I took a stroll. In the courtyard of the Kona Hilton sat a tall beautiful red, white, green and yellow macaw with a beak that looked as dangerous as a Samurai sword. It sat atop its perch as proudly as any monarch sitting on his throne. His eyes seemed to be able to look into your very soul. People admired him from afar, reverently observing the warning sign, "DO NOT ATTEMPT TO PET THIS BIRD. ITS BEAK CAN SNAP A ONE-INCH STICK."

Having owned two parrots, David had developed a sense of communication with birds that was unusual for a boy of fourteen. Undaunted by the warning, David went up to the large macaw on their first encounter and demanded, "Raise your wing and let me scratch you." The large bird quickly raised his right wing. David bravely scratched it. The bird was in seventh heaven. "Now the other one," boomed David's voice. The left wing was up and the bird nearly purred. "Lower your head so I can scratch it!" ordered David's young voice. Entranced by the voice, the bird became his puppet. This routine occurred every time we passed his domain. In a hurry one day, David started to pass up his friend, when that bird let out the loudest bellow of complaint we had ever heard. I don't think we could have continued if David hadn't given him a few minutes of the physical therapy he had learned to love. He was so contented he nearly fell off his perch.

On our last morning there, David wanted to make one final visit to say goodbye to his friend. Unfortunately, there were others watching him from afar. As David went through various commands, the crowd drew closer. The scene enthralled one young boy. His father tried to draw him away several times, but the boy was glued to the spot. As David said his last goodbye, the bird seemed to understand. He made the strangest moan and turned his head from side to side. I thought I saw tears in his eyes. I know Dave's and my eyes had tears in them. It was evident that David had indeed made a friend.

As we were walking away, the young boy started prodding his dad to scratch the bird's head. As they stepped within the boundaries of his domain, the bird leaned forward and barely missed biting the man. Backing off, the crowd showed the proper respect, and we walked around to the front door. After loading our boxes of fresh pineapples and luggage, I drove the family in the rental car back to the airport.

Four hours later, the giant mechanical bird lifted off the runway, and headed for Chicago. The beautiful boats on the blue water become smaller and smaller as we climbed higher and higher.

Chapter 11

We Checked Out Barrier Free

AT LAST—BARRIER FREE

WHEN WE TOOK David and Susan to Washington D.C., we went to most of the tourist attractions Dave had always wanted to see. Before he worked on the National Barrier-Free Architectural and Transportation Board with Senator Bob Dole, it was impossible for a person in a wheelchair to enter the national monuments. When Dave and the kids stood in line to go to the Washington Monument, the park ranger went over and had them enter immediately. By the time I parked the car and returned, they had been to the top where they enjoyed the view from the small windows, and were on their way down.

Dave and I were pleased to talk to many people in wheelchairs who were finally able to join their families in the Washington, Lincoln and Jefferson monuments, and other national sights they had always wanted to see, but couldn't access until then. When I told them Dave was on the committee that helped make them accessible, they asked him many questions. We loved reading the wonderful words on the walls of the monuments. They let American and foreign tourists know that this country was indeed founded on belief in God.

We made an interesting observation the first time Dave was able to go up into the Lincoln Memorial in Washington D.C. We followed a sidewalk to a wheelchair accessible door that is located on the side of the Memorial foundation base. To enter the elevator, we were facing the underside of the Memorial. When we were in the area under the monument, we were amazed to see that the bottom of the thick cement, which makes up the floor of the Memorial, has a large number of huge stalactites hanging from the ceiling and massive stalagmites covering the floor in the entire cavity under the monument. They reminded us of those located in the Ohio and Carlsbad Caverns, where the kids and I were told the stalactites and stalagmites are thousands of years old. The Lincoln Monument was probably less than one hundred years old. It was a good lesson for the kids and us to not believe everything we're told.

At the White House, we were escorted to a different entrance. There were many guards there. We looked past the guards. We were able to wave back to the President Carter's daughter and grandchildren who were out in the yard playing. It was a pleasant surprise. The area was surrounded by trees which provided privacy from the view of the public. Many tourists stood along the fence that separated them from this very public, but private, residence. Everyone hoped to catch a glimpse of a member of the First Family.

The hotel we stayed in was across from the Pentagon. It was fun to watch the helicopters land on the lawn of the Pentagon, and wonder who was exiting or entering the door. We planned to walk around the area for about an hour while our teenagers were swimming. When we came back, we took the elevator up to the pool. I went to tell the kids we would eat soon. Suddenly the smoke alarms went off. Dave was blocking the door of the elevator so it would wait for me. I ran back to tell Dave the kids weren't there. We took the elevator down to our floor. Again, I ran to our room to find them while Dave was holding the elevator. They weren't there. We took the elevator downstairs. As we exited the elevator, many firemen wearing full gear greeted us; they took the elevator to the area of the reported smoke. The firemen soon returned on the elevator. A cigarette butt had ignited some sheets and pillowcases in the closet of soiled linen. The fire was out when they arrived. The elevator could be used again.

We continued searching for our teenagers; hotel employees hadn't seen them; finally, David and Susan were in the lobby. They saw the fire trucks and were afraid something might have happened to one of us. They had walked over a mile to eat a pizza at an Italian restaurant they had spotted when we were driving to the hotel. They said the pizza was great. We were proud of the kids for being so resourceful. A few days later, when we turned the TV on in New York City, we saw on the news that two men had been shot in that DC restaurant by drive-by professionals. A million thoughts went through our minds of what could have been.

EMBARRASSING MOMENTS

One of our most embarrassing moments on any trip had to be the time we stayed in the New York Hilton. Remembering the nice laundry rooms in the Hilton and Sheraton Hotels in Hawaii the year before, we made the mistake of assuming that all Hiltons would have a laundry room available. When I asked if we could wash our clothes there, the bellhop, thinking that I meant valet service, agreed that we could. We had two large black lawn bags full of dirty laundry. The bellboy removed them from our van, and placed the black bags beside our matching luggage on the large cart.

When we registered, we were told that the wheelchair-accessible room that Dave had reserved, was unavailable because the guest using that room on the night before, decided to stay two additional nights. We were shuffled around to three or four other rooms, each with a bathroom door too narrow for the wheelchair to enter.

Businessmen and women, wearing their thousand-dollar, plus, suits were in the lobby registering. Our luggage and ugly black plastic bags, bulging with dirty clothes, had been unloaded and reloaded on the cart in each room we had visited. The manager finally came out of his office and offered to have us stay at the Waldorf Astoria. Dave explained that the last time we had stayed there, the entrance was not barrier-free. The hotel staff person who assisted in carrying him up the steps to the Waldorf, tripped, and Dave had nearly been dropped. Because of that remembrance, he refused the offer.

As we stood talking in the lobby, one of the black bags fell off the cart. When the bellhop grabbed the bag by its side, it burst open, and out poured many dirty, sweaty clothes. The young employee was embarrassed and went to find another plastic bag. In the meantime, the contents of the broken bag got the full attention of most guests standing there. One of the exquisitely dressed women watching was especially nice. She came over, looked at the pile, then to me, and gave me a hug. When she announced, quite loudly, "Everyone has now viewed your dirty laundry in public," everyone had a good laugh. It broke the ice, but Dave and I asked to speak to the manager privately, while the bellhop filled a new plastic bag. Dave reminded the manager that he had made this reservation six months earlier, and had been promised an accessible room. The manager was visibly flustered when Dave asked him if a hotel this large only had one wheelchair accessible room. Before the man could answer the question, Dave reminded him that we had reservations to a Broadway show.

I proceeded to tell the manager about the committees Dave was serving on to check out wheelchair accessibility nation-wide. I explained that the government was interested in knowing if hotels, large or small, had adequate rooms available to serve the public's needs. I smiled, but I made him aware that no guest appreciates being embarrassed in front of other guests in the lobby of such a distinguished hotel. I mentioned that Dave was one of the liaisons with Senator Bob Dole, and this incident would be reported to his office when we returned from this trip. The grin on his face quickly disappeared and he nicely apologized to Dave. He had the bellhop take our luggage to a nice large room for us to change so we could go to the Broadway play on time. Dave could not enter the bathroom of the large room, so the kids had to go to the lobby while Dave changed. Dave told the manager that, since he had offered us the opportunity to transfer to the Waldorf, he would note his generosity in his report. When we left the hotel, the doorman greeted us personally.

The doorman left other guests standing, and gave us the next taxi. That may sound nice, but the driver was furious because he was next in line to get a fare to Kennedy Airport. At first he refused to take us, but when the doorman went up to the driver's side of the taxi, we heard him quietly tell the driver we were VIP's, and threatened to not let him come into the hotel driveway if he wasn't nice to us. He told the driver he was to take us to the theatre, and then return. The doorman assured him he wouldn't have to wait in line, but would get the next Kennedy Airport fare. The driver apologized and explained it to us on the way to the theatre. When we saw how close the theatre was to the hotel, Dave gave the man a generous tip. The four of us walked back to the hotel that evening.

When we returned to the hotel, the manager proudly told us we would be staying in the penthouse. He explained he had confirmed that Goodwill Industries of America, a U.S. Senator, and several Michigan legislators knew Dave. He told us many confidential facts he had learned about us. It frightened us to know that, on a Friday night, a hotel could obtain this information, including the fact that our daughter was an air traffic controller in the U.S. Navy, serving on Guam. This was in 1979, before the usage of today's computers. Big Brother was already at work.

We were shown to the lovely penthouse. It was half of the two top floors of the hotel, and was tastefully decorated in Oriental. There was a full-size grand piano, several seating areas, and a large fireplace in the living room; the dining room must have seated twenty; there were four or five bedrooms and many large bathrooms. There was a winding stairway between the floors, as well as a lovely private elevator. We had a private maid named Julie. I'm sure the hotel had her there to protect the lovely penthouse that was used by many famous people. Julie told us that the stairway in the living room was the scene of many lovely weddings by famous people.

Dave chose a large room with only one king size bed in it for the two of us. It overlooked Central Park. We were able to look down at men and women sunbathing on the penthouse terraces. We were surprised at how many mature trees (some at least twenty stories high) there are on some of those rooftop terraces.

Dave Davey talking to a performer at the Medieval Times show

When Dave planned to watch the news in our room, the TV didn't work. Within five minutes after Dave called Room Service, the TV repairman was there. He asked Dave where we lived. Dave told the young man we lived in Portage, Michigan, but Dave let him know he was originally from a city near Detroit, Michigan. The man said he had heard of some of the areas Dave mentioned, but he had never been there. When he asked about me, Dave laughed and said, "Indiana, but I don't think you've heard of the town." When the repairman asked Dave what the name of the town was, he replied, "New Richmond." Dave couldn't believe it when the man quickly said, "Oh, I've been there." Dave smiled and tried to convince him that he had probably been to Richmond since New Richmond has less than four hundred residents. The man laughed and said, "I remember New Richmond. It has a hitching post in front of the Building and Loan, one flashing light, with a furniture store, restaurant, grocery store, and a hardware store located on the four corners." That was a very accurate description of New Richmond at the time. The repairman also told about the restaurant in a small village four miles away that had the best hamburgers he had ever eaten. It wasn't long after our trip when the movie "Hoosiers" (filmed in and around New Richmond) was released. We have wondered if the TV repairman was somehow connected to the movie.

We were told later that when Gene Hackman, the star of "Hoosiers" met Mrs. Stephens, manager of the New Richmond Post Office, she told him that she and his mother were best friends in Illinois when they were young women. She showed him pictures of them together. Because all of Gene's mother's pictures were burned in a house fire, he was thrilled to see the pictures, and borrowed them to have copies made.

Of course I never let Dave forget that people in New York know where New Richmond is, but not the Detroit area cities where he grew up. Dave decided that since New Richmond appeared to be so well known, he would never again tease me about the one flashing-light town. However, he still loved to tease me about Coal Creek Central, the high school where I graduated. Dave and my uncles called it a large chicken coop. Dave never let me forget it.

Dave grew a beard for 8 weeks after he lost bet with Anne

From the penthouse, we looked down on the lovely horse drawn carriages, known as taxis, going through Central Park. Dave had always wanted to ride through Central Park in a carriage, but didn't consider it possible because he didn't want anyone to injure his or her back lifting him. David and I didn't think there would be any problem to get him onto a carriage. The next day we went to the park. I asked a driver if his taxi (carriage) was barrier free. He laughed and assured us it was. The other drivers of the lovely horse driven taxis said they would watch Dave's wheelchair while we were gone.

Two drivers and David easily lifted Dave up onto the front seat. We were thrilled to see the lovely landscaping of Central Park. There was a concert on the right side of the road, and people roller-skating beside the taxi. Sure enough, Dave's wheelchair was there when we returned. There were many volunteers to assist in getting him back into the wheelchair. That ride was one of Dave's favorite memories.

On Sunday morning we ate brunch at Sybil's, a lovely restaurant in the New York Hilton. The meal was part of our package. A lovely blonde woman came over, introduced herself as Sybil, and apologized because Dave couldn't reach some of the food in the center of the large table. Never had Dave nor I ever seen such a choice of gourmet brunch items. After I carried Dave's plate, the owner came over to our table and asked Dave what kind of dessert he'd prefer. She asked one of the waiters to bring over the large dessert cabinet. The choices were mind-boggling. Dave asked her to choose one for him, but asked her if he was allowed to take it with him since it was a brunch. She said she would pack one for each of us. She asked what we wanted. Susan, David, and I asked her to choose any one for us as well. About thirty minutes later, while we were still eating, she came over with a tray full of the most delicious delicacies we ever tasted. They were neatly covered for our travel. At that time, we were once again reminded that being in a wheelchair sometimes does have its advantages.

Chapter 12

Progress Continues

$\mathcal{W}$HEN KEN SHAW left Kalamazoo to become the Director of Rehabilitation and Educative Services at Goodwill Industries International, Dennis (Denny) Frey accepted the position of Associate Executive Director. Denny Frey and Ken Shaw had worked as a CARF accreditation team when Ken worked for Dave, and Denny worked at a private workshop in Pennsylvania. Ken felt Denny was the perfect person for the position. Denny had many fresh ideas for providing needed services. He proved to be a good partner, and continued to add strong team players to the staff.

During that time, the government finally realized that all people deserved an opportunity to work, and the United States was introduced to the "Rehabilitation Explosion." Goodwill established partnerships with Michigan Vocational Rehabilitation Services, Blind Services, and most other funding agencies. Kalamazoo was the first Goodwill to have a talking computer for blind clients. Grants allowed us to serve the more severely handicapped people. Our service areas expanded beyond previous dreams of Dave and the staff. Goodwill's programs branched out to serving at-risk younger people, refugees, parolees, and the list continued to grow. These breakthroughs marked the first time government agencies in Michigan engaged in workforce development activities with a local Goodwill. One project that was specifically developed to target serving high school students, also partnered with Kalamazoo Valley Community College. Dave and Denny Frey were always searching for the best programs available. Computers were constantly being upgraded.

Denny Frey wrote a grant for some upscale industrial equipment, including a router. The one million famous "Massage Pets" designed and owned by Creative Wood Specialties, Inc. were manufactured exclusively in Goodwill's industrial program. This contract created many work areas for on-the-job training of our clients.

Galyn Barnum joined the staff at Goodwill Industries of Southwestern Michigan in 1983. She was hired by Carla Fallon. What an addition! Carla was the Psychologist at Goodwill, and provided psychiatric evaluations for Michigan Vocational Rehabilitation clients to determine their readiness to benefit from Job Training, Interview Skill Training, and other programs that could place developmentally disabled persons onto jobs at their skill level. Galyn was hired to do job evaluations, but her outstanding abilities were quickly recognized. She soon became the Goodwill Director of Vocational Services. Galyn was invaluable to Goodwill. Galyn recently told me that Dave was instrumental in setting the vision that people should not just move off the welfare rolls, but should become fully engaged in their community. Dave felt it was the responsibility of the local Goodwill to eliminate barriers to make that vision possible. Galyn said Dave shared that philosophy with everyone in rehabilitation. Dave often met with Bob Straits, Director of Kalamazoo-St. Joseph Michigan WORKS! to discuss Goodwill's involvement with the different programs that were planned for the future. As Dave and Bob Straits met, Denny Frey and Galyn Barnum were busy preparing for Michigan WORKS! This Welfare to Work program was designed to get recipients off welfare rolls.

Dave was elected to the Goodwill Industries International's Executive Council from 1984 to 1987. As chairman of the Conference of Executives in 1986 and 1987, Dave used the opportunity to promote open sharing and the exchange of ideas across the Goodwill movement. The phones began to ring. Once encouraged to share, most Goodwills were excited to be participating in the philosophy of national networking. It was the perfect time for Dave to contact other CEOs for their input. He used input from the Michigan Goodwill CEOs, and the Michigan Goodwill Association (now GAM) was established.

David Cooney, CEO of Goodwill Industries International, called and asked Dave to serve as the liaison for the Goodwill family regarding the passage of the Americans with Disabilities Act. In this endeavor, Dave often talked with Senator Bob Dole. Dave felt they had become friends when they served as members of the National Architectural Barrier and Transportation Board. America was ready for it to happen.

During the beginning of one program, a young woman came into the lobby pushing her baby stroller when Dave was talking to the Goodwill receptionist. When Dave welcomed the young woman to Goodwill, she groused about preferring to be home watching soap operas instead of wasting her time at Goodwill. Just then, one of her friends came out of class on a break. She was a participant in the program. She came over and gave the young mother a hug. She told the new woman that she would love the training once she had self-respect. The new participant argued that she had self-respect, let her friend know she would never enjoy the training, and continued to vent her frustrations. Dave saw both women several times during their training period. About two years later when Dave and I were shopping, the woman with the baby came up to us and gave us big hugs. She proudly told us that she was a student at Kalamazoo Valley College at night, and had a good job. She was supporting her baby and herself quite nicely, and was finally off food stamps. She said that she wouldn't be having any more babies out of wedlock because she had too much self-respect to go down that road again. She told Dave several times to thank the Goodwill staff for all they had done for her.

Chapter 13

Conference Of Executives

HEN DAVE LEARNED he was chairman of the 1986 Conference of Executives, he was so pleased the Conference would be at the New Orleans Goodwill with Jim Collins, President, hosting. His wife, Pat, was one of my favorite spouses. She and I discussed inviting all the spouses to accompany the executives to New Orleans. Pat sent an invitation to every one of the spouses, urging them to join their husband or wife. Many of them were pleased to know they were allowed to attend. We learned that, in the past, many were not notified by their spouse that there was organized entertainment for the spouses, resulting in only a few wives attending. When others had attended, they often kept to themselves. In the past, I only knew Bev Cooney, Pat Collins, Ouida Hoke, and Pat Wisecarver. Pat Collins received a wonderful response and began making great plans for our time there.

Dave, Mom Simpson, and Anne on plane to New Orleans Conference of Executives

After much persuasion, Dave's mom, Helen Simpson, went with us. She was quite impressed when a limousine met us at the airport, and Goodwill International had reserved a wonderful room for us. We were next to the Hospitality Room where we could eat nearly anything, at nearly any time of the day or night. When we visited the Hospitality Room for the first time, the attendant greeted us with, "Welcome David, Anne, and Helen." Mom told Dave that she could understand why we loved going to the Conference of Executives. Dave explained that, it was only because he was chairman that year, that we were given that room. Dave had to attend meetings during the day all week.

We joined several other Goodwill executives and spouses on the first night to attend Pete Fountain's Jazz Club. The music was wonderful. Pete came over to our table where he was introduced to Dave and others during his break time. He urged Mom and me to watch the floats the next morning, and promised that he would throw us some beads and coins. He explained that each person in the parade who throws the different items is responsible for buying them. Mom and I attended Dave's first breakfast business meeting long enough for Dave to introduce Mom. When anyone saw Mom during the week, they pleased her when they yelled, "Hello Mom!"

We had a fun breakfast with the spouses on the Streetcar named Desire, the streetcar made famous by the 1951 movie, starring Marlon

Brando and Vivian Leigh. (Vivian won the Best Actress for her role; but Marlon, nominated for a Best Actor Oscar for his role, lost.)

After breakfast, Mom and I went down the street two blocks to watch the first of the parades. On the right side of where we were standing sat a large flat wagon with seats holding about thirty military men. Several families and individuals stood around us. One man sat on the top board of the white wood fence at the edge of the parade route. The loud jazz bands foretold us of the floats coming around the corner. There was Pete Fountain on one of the lead floats. He smiled and yelled, "Hello Mom and Anne. These are for you," and threw a large bag of bead necklaces toward us. However, the bag was quickly intercepted by the man who was standing on the fence. He put them in a backpack he was wearing. Pete was obviously disgusted and yelled for him to give them to us. The man ignored him. Pete threw a bag of coins toward us. Again, the man reached up and grabbed them in the air to deposit them in his backpack. By that time, Pete's float was out of sight. One by one the man was grabbing beads intended for someone in the audience. Mom yelled at the floaters to just throw one or two strands at a time. We each caught about ten. We drew back to allow others to get closer. By that time, the man had grabbed fifteen or twenty bags that the thrower had designated for others. The crowd was getting angry, and screaming at the man on the fence. Mom suggested we should get out of there and go back to our hotel.

When we returned to our room, I turned on the TV. The TV was showing the military men and other members of the crowd we had just left. The man was not on the fence, but the announcer shocked us when he told about a bystander who went up and stabbed a man on the fence because the man had grabbed a bag that was meant to be his. The announcer said it was the first death of Mardi gras. Needless to say, we did not attend any more of the parades. During the week, the spouses visited a plantation, toured the city and saw many other sites that have been made famous by movies.

One evening there was a private concert by the New Orleans Jazz Club in the large Concert Hall across from the hotel. One of their members presented Dave with a lovely "THE NEW ORLEANS JAZZ CLUB 1983, 35th Anniversary '48–'83" poster which continues to hang on my office wall at home.

As we were returning to the hotel, two men in their twenties came out of nowhere, and were zooming down the street toward us on their bicycles. One man grabbed Ouida Hoke's purse out of her hand. The other bicyclist pushed Pete Hoke onto the ground, and purposely broke his glasses as Pete was chasing him. Others joined Pete in pursuit of the men, but the bicycles were out of sight immediately. We knew it had to be someone who had seen Ouida with her very valuable antique turquoise and silver jewelry the night before. They also had to know that she kept the jewelry in her purse, and not in a safe in the hotel. The jewelry had been a wedding gift from Pete more than fifty years before. I never heard if the police or insurance company retrieved the jewelry.

When most of us went out to a famous plantation used in movies, Mom stayed at the hotel, and was a guest on a TV cook show. The next evening, we had dinner aboard the paddle boat on the Mississippi River. Jim Collins had the captain present a certificate naming Dave as Honorary Captain of the ship, signed by the Captain.

Jim Collins, CEO of New Orleans Goodwill and Anne Davey watch Dave show the Key to New Orleans to other CEOs at Conference of Execs

On the last day, Jim Collins presented Dave with a Proclamation from the Governor of Louisiana making Dave an officer on his staff, and a certificate which gave Dave the keys to the City of New Orleans, signed by the Mayor.

Pat and Jim had thought of everything. They were delightful people.

Chapter 14

And Life Goes On

*O*N GOOD FRIDAY, March 25, 1989, Dave suffered respiratory failure. An ambulance rushed him to Bronson Hospital. While there, his lungs were attacked by several different infections. Most of the infections were unknown to the laboratories in several states that examined the samples. Dave spent the next sixty-three days in Bronson Hospital, under the care of Drs. Abraham, Dircks, Grambau, and Schoell, a team of caring and capable pulmonary specialists. After a short time, Dave had a tracheotomy. He spent many weeks on a respirator. The respiratory therapists spent much time draining his lungs of the infections. Near the end of his stay, a respiratory therapist told Dave that sixty-three patients had died of those infections in Bronson's Intensive Care Unit during his stay. None of those who died was a patient of Dave's medical team.

The hours I spent at the hospital during Dave's respiratory failure were overwhelming. Any time I wasn't working, I spent at Bronson with Dave. Nearly every time he awoke, I was there holding his hand. I brought aloe lotion from home and rubbed it on Dave to prevent bedsores that troubled many patients. I went home at midnight and was back at Dave's side by six a.m. I assisted in his care wherever I was allowed. With so many extremely ill patients there, the medical teams welcomed my help.

We appreciated the good care Dave was getting, so every three days I brought flowers, baskets of fruit, boxes of candy, cherry pies I baked at night, and other items for the great staff.

Once when Dave was recovering, I went into his room with a bouquet of Tootsie Pops. He asked me what I was going to do with them because he didn't think anyone there would eat them. I took them to the nurse's station, and within five minutes everyone who came into Dave's room had one in his or her mouth. Dave loved it.

More importantly, Dave said I gave him the love and moral support that he needed to motivate him to get well. He had a reason to live. The doctors and nurses were afraid I would wear myself out and catch something from the many ill patients, but God sustained me. Our daughter, Susan, was an occupational therapist at the hospital and she visited Dave. Otherwise, no visitor was allowed in his room. During most of his stay, he was in Intensive Care. A few hours after Dave returned home from the hospital, we listened to "60 Minutes". A pathologist told about the infections Dave had. He reported there had been thousands of deaths from those unknown lung infections in the United States in two months. God spared Dave once again. Dave and I thanked God that he had the best doctors, equipment, respiratory therapists and nurses anywhere.

Dave also thanked God that Denny Frey was willing to be the Acting Director of Goodwill for about six months. He and other staff members ran the agency very well. For three months after Dave returned home, he had a visiting nurse with him from 7:30 a.m. to 4:45 p.m. Monday through Friday while I was at work. Dave liked to tell me that his 4:45 p.m. to 7:30 a.m. nurse was his favorite.

The following year, at Goodwill's annual meeting, I sat with the husband of one of Goodwill's board members. It turned out that he was the pathologist who had sent samples of liquid from Dave's lungs to laboratories across America, to identify the infections. Some of those infections were new to science, but he told me those were the same infections that killed Jim Henson, the creator of the Muppets.

After being on medical leave for five months, Dave returned to Goodwill part-time for a few weeks, then full time. His energy level never fully recovered, so he worked only forty hours a week. Dr. Abraham requested Dave to buy a van before he would allow him to return to work. Vocational Rehabilitation Services was allowed to help with the cost of the van because that was the only way Dave would be allowed to work; we were so grateful, and Dave appreciated the van. Not having to get into the car, pull his chair into the back seat, and move over to close the door, saved so much energy, and I'm sure it prolonged his life considerably.

Helen Simpson, Marilyn (Dave's sister) and Stan Zidel, Bill Louden, Board member, Max (Dave's brother) and Margaret Davey, James and Susan Gibson at Dave's Goodwill Roast

Chapter 15

I Made It To Sixty

Dave wrote this chapter shortly after his retirement in 2000.

IN 1996, ANNE and Susan planned the most memorable surprise party anyone could have for their sixtieth birthday. Mom had talked with Anne and Susan about the fact that I had lived such a full life. She encouraged them to have a big party when I was sixty in case she, my friends, or I didn't live long enough to celebrate my sixty-fifth birthday. Mom died in 1995 when the party was still in the planning stage.

Our son David flew in from Washington D.C. Anne's nieces, Dr. Janet Lerner, and Janet's sister and brother-in-law, Drs. Martha and Haakon Smith, flew in from New York City. Friends flew in from Tucson, Arizona, several Michigan and Indiana cities, and many drove in from other cities and states. It was held a week before I was sixty.

Susan Gibson and Anne Davey share
the story of Crumbs in the Butter

My brother Max was the emcee. The entertainment lasted more than two hours. Our family members are musically talented. There was singing, instrumental solos, poems, funny stories, and a sentimental tape of Mom's and my talking together in 1994. We talked about Mom when she was young, and nostalgia about my family. Three singers in our family have wonderful soprano voices. Our daughter Susan and my sister Marilyn, each sang beautiful songs. It brought tears to my eyes when each brought the mike over to have me accompany her for the last few lines. Anne's niece, Martha, sings opera and Christian music in New York and Europe. She received a standing ovation as she sang "Holy City". Haakon is an accomplished concert pianist and played piano solos, as well as accompanying Martha and the crowd as they sang. My nephew David Zidel played trombone solos and my niece Jennifer Zidel a flute solo. God was truly honored. The entire event was captured on videos. Videos of the party were played on the local cable channel at three different times.

One of the stories that Susan and Anne told at the party was about my love for Susan's chocolate chip cookies and Anne's cherry pies.

Dave Davey showing friends the Crumbs in the
Butter at his 60th birthday party

We were scheduled to go to Mackinac Island the following week. While I was sound asleep, Anne got up at 3:00 a.m. and baked a cherry pie, cooled it, and packed it in the back of the van the day we left for Mackinac City. Susan baked chocolate chip cookies. When we got to the hotel, it was the night before our reservations for the Grand Hotel on Mackinac Island. When I heard about the cherry pie, it really surprised me. I couldn't believe that I could sleep through the smell of a cherry pie baking. Anne told me she had closed our bedroom door, opened the window, and turned on the exhaust fan. I loved their delight in surprising me.

Dave Davey arriving at the Grand Hotel on Mackinac Island, Michigan

Chapter 16

Caring Friends Gone Home

ALBERT FESMIRE WENT TO BE WITH THE LORD

IT WAS A great loss to Dave when Albert Fesmire, Dave's long-time friend, confidant, and pastor, went home to be with the Lord. Pastor Fesmire had visited Dave frequently in Kalamazoo when Dave went through difficult times in his life. Pastor Fesmire and his lovely wife Margie left the Battle Creek Bible Church when Albert became pastor of a church in Richmond, Virginia. We visited them there. Dave enjoyed talking with Pastor Fesmire long distance until the pastor's illness prevented it.

GOD TOOK DAVE'S MOM HOME

Mom was more than a mother to us. She was an advisor, true friend, counselor, encourager and Christian example. When Mom's beloved husband Bill was dying of cancer, Mom was diagnosed with breast cancer. Aware she was risking her life, but not wanting to worry Bill, Mom waited the life-threatening months until Bill died before having the breast removed. Dave called Mom for two hours or more every Saturday after that. I talked to her during the week. Mom had to sell her car and quit driving her friends to their favorite pie restaurant because she was diagnosed with macular degeneration. She continued to teach her Bible classes, using a lighted magnifying glass. After her other breast was removed, the cancer returned. She was exhausted and refused to take chemo or any other treatment. She looked forward to death so she could be with the Lord. The nurses and other staff at the hospital saw her great faith and asked her to tell them about Jesus as she lay dying. Dave's sister, Marilyn, called and allowed us to speak to Mom as she lay dying in the hospital. Once she died, Marilyn, Dave's brother Max, and the hospital employees had a prayer circle around her. I still miss our talks.

*Dave with Stan, Cindy, sister Marilyn and
Jennifer Zidel after Mom's funeral*

ROOMMATE'S DESTINY FULFILLED

Dick Wooten, Dave's roommate at Wayne State University, transferred with Goodwill Industries to California in the 1960's. He and his wife, Pat, later developed a business of large-scale national accessible equipment shows. Within a short time, the participants included large manufacturers & suppliers. The shows encouraged the development of more and better accessible equipment. Dave often called Dick for his advice or to congratulate him when Dave read something about Dick in a national magazine. When Dick heard about what Dave and Ken Shaw were developing, he called Dave to congratulate him on the successful rehabilitation programs he and Ken were sharing with others. Dave and Dick were delighted that they were seeing their college dreams come to fruition. Each of their accomplishments motivated the other to succeed.

A relaxing visit from Pat and Dick Wooten
(Dave's roommate at Wayne State University)

When Dick and Pat Wooten visited us in the 1990's, they showed us the mini-van they drove. It was equipped with everything imaginable. The entire bottom of the van lowered to allow Dick, on his chair, to enter the van, then raised back up to allow him to drive it. When they saw Dave's full size van, fully equipped to serve all of his needs, Dick and Pat told us they had worked with many manufacturers during the development stage of Dave's accessible equipment. Dave and Dick were amazed as they compared notes on what each of them felt their destiny was in the 1950's. God had allowed both of them to accomplish most of the goals they set in their dorm room at Wayne State.

Dick and Pat's shows had become such a huge, successful business that they later sold their business for millions. They were to attend the shows for a few years, but Dick died unexpectedly in 1995. The loss of a long-time true friend and confidante was hard for Dave. Dick had been a sounding board for Dave on so many thoughts and ideas that helped change America's view of people in chairs. Dick's life, like Dave's, was spent improving the lives of all people with disabilities. What a blessing for wheelchair users worldwide that Dave, Dick and Pat pursued their purpose in life.

Chapter 17

We Drove North To Alaska

$\mathcal{M}$Y MIND OFTEN goes back to the wonderful trip Dave and I took to Alaska in 1999. Dave appreciated getting to plan that trip for a year. Everywhere we traveled, it was evident that he had done a superb job.

A lifetime dream of seeing Alaska came true in 1999. Dave and I spent nearly three months together, seeing the northwestern part of the United States. We were able to see some of the most beautiful scenery of our great country. Between here and there, we saw magnificent mountains, the famous Badlands, Mt. Rushmore and Yellowstone National Park.

Dennis and Janet (Dave's sister) Hatfield in Nebraska

On our way from Portage, Michigan to Bellingham, Washington to catch the Alaskan ship AMHS Columbia, we spent Saturday and Sunday nights in Mitchell, South Dakota. We attended church at Calvary Baptist Church. Their building is wheelchair accessible. The teaching was great. We took the pastor and his wife, Robert and Sandy Conner, to dinner. Robert told us he had been diagnosed with cancer ten months before. At the same time, Sandy had been told she was two months pregnant. Robert was given less than three months to live. When Dave told him we wanted to take them out to lunch on our way back home in twelve weeks, Robert told Dave that he didn't expect to be alive then. Dave surprised me when he told Robert he would be alive when we returned because God just told him that Robert would not die in 1999.

In the Badlands, many trails are wheelchair accessible. We were surprised as we followed the paths to discover that these were not stone mountains, but hills comprised of dried mud that flaked off. We examined the chunks kicked off by children who followed their parents up the slopes.

Mt. Rushmore was nice, and as we drove through forests on the one-way drive, we discovered the many ways these regal faces are shown at their best. What a thrill it was to see them at the end of tunnels, or framed by trees cut out at a turn in the road. We also saw a buffalo walking around the cars in a gas station, white horned sheep eating beside our car, wild burros that looked in our window as we photographed them, and other animals native to the area.

In Yellowstone, it was interesting to learn that an earthquake changed the faithfulness of Old Faithful's eruption to approximately every 88 minutes. We were able to see herds of buffalo, elk, prong-horned antelope, foxes, and coyotes.

Later, when Dave looked up at a very high mountain cliff, he pulled the van off the highway. The sight of a mother mountain goat teaching her twins to jump a great distance from one cliff to another, was awesome. We were amazed at the patience of the mother goat. Her first kid jumped on the second try, and stood still while he and his mother waited for his brother to follow suit. They watched while the second kid would start, then stop at the very edge of the cliff. The mother returned to the other side about four times. The last time she was standing next to the anxious kid, she grabbed his fur by the scruff of his neck, and shook him. We were surprised, that with her being hundreds of feet above us, we could hear her when she let out the loudest goat call we had ever heard. She looked at the kid, turned, and jumped and he quickly followed her. The mother and the kid's brother gently rubbed heads with him, apparently giving him support of a jump well done. In a flash, they were out of sight.

I walked into the woods and took close-up movies of a huge bull elk. I calmly walked back to the van as the elk started stomping his feet and snorting within a few feet of my camera. Dave held his camera in hand, shooting the site from the van. We quickly left the scene.

ALASKA, AT LAST

Dave and I appreciated taking helicopters so we could see places we never could have traveled to otherwise. Dave said it made him feel so blessed and special that God would allow us to see Alaska as few have seen it.

Dave Davey eating in the dining room on the Alaskan Marine Highway.

In Alaska, we visited glaciers from helicopters and special tour boats. Dave couldn't get out of the helicopter during our trip, but I found it exciting to walk on the edge of a glacier where the helicopter landed on a small patch of ice. With the special "boots" passengers are required to wear to prevent slipping on the ice, I was able to stand near the glacier's edge and look down twelve hundred feet.

Later it was fun watching large chunks of ice as it fell from the face of a glacier, sending the boat bobbing in the water. Huge icebergs, hundreds of growlers, and chunks of ice occupied by seals and sea otters, floated by. Binoculars made them easy to see. As the boat often took a noisy beating from the ice below, we were reminded of the Titanic. The ice is a crystal clear sea blue that is unique to glaciers. Although we were told the glacier ice is thousands of years old, when they melted it inside the boat, we were surprised to see it was full of worms that swam as soon as they were freed from the ice. Even so, some tourists tasted the water from the melted ice, worms included.

Dave and Anne Davey on an Alaskan ship. Anne
couldn't get a good shot of the rapidly flowing water,
so she shot the reflection in the windows.

We sailed the Inside Passage and across the Gulf of Alaska, using the State owned Alaska Marine Highway System (AMHS). We enjoyed a cabin as well as having our van on board. Since I am afraid of heights, we shared the bottom berth, varying from thirty-four to thirty-nine inches wide, on three of the ships we sailed. Many passengers slept on deck in tents taped to the deck with duct tape. Others slept on deck chairs in the Solarium. We visited Barrow, Dutch Harbor, Haines, Homer, Hope, Juneau, Ketchikan, Pelican Island, Petersburg, Seward, Skagway, Valdez and Wrangell.

Dave Davey asked all ship staff to sign our "Alaska Trip" book

At Ketchikan, we were allowed to drive our van off during the three-hour visit. Dave asked a young staff person who lived there if he would be willing to act as our guide. He was a native and took us to the Totem Pole Village, only two blocks from the house where he was raised as a child. His explanation of the history and meaning behind each totem was so interesting that the tourists from the Princess Tours moved from their guide and listened to our young friend as we heard about his ancestors. His wife told us that her husband's grandfather had carved many of the totems. One interesting story was about the village honoring Abraham Lincoln, but with only a photo from his waist up, they carved a totem with very short legs. There were other totems carved to dishonor people who had received many nice gifts from the tribe, but had not reciprocated in like manner.

After we left Wrangell, the captain announced we would be going through the famous Wrangell Narrows. The AMHS Columbia is the largest passenger ship allowed to pass through these waters. The ship can only pass through the narrow, shallow channel during high tide. A second officer was posted as lookout at the front of the ship as the captain carefully zigzagged through the tight channel with only a few feet of water under the ship to separate it from going aground. The passengers were silent as they watched from the front windows or stood on the deck. Sighs of relief were heard as we cleared the final turn. Murmurs of agreement followed one young passenger's comment, "That was more fun than a roller coaster."

In Juneau, we drove our van to the lovely two-bedroom apartment Dave had rented for the week. Later we enjoyed an afternoon at the top of the Tramway. An eagle chose to clean itself on a treetop just about twenty-five or thirty feet from us. What a delight to see the huge wings spread out as it cleaned each feather. It would often turn itself around, sometimes seeming to try to out-stare the cameras focused intently on it's every movement. The Juneau team of hang-gliders also entertained us as they sailed their bodies up and around the mountain. Their colorful kites above them picked up the winds and currents.

After we saw the eagle, Dave drove to the Juneau glacier. I pushed him to the end of the walk that goes within one-hundred-plus feet of ice from the glacier. When we started, the path was very warm, but as we neared the glacier, Dave put on the coat he brought. The area around the ice was very cold. We couldn't believe that we were that close to a glacier.

There was a nice restaurant across the parking lot from our apartment. Upon returning from the glacier, we went there to eat. As we sat talking, a woman came in, introduced herself as a state legislator, and sat down to share our table. She was a very interesting person. Dave asked her how the food was there because we had been warned not to eat eggs and many other food items in Alaska. She laughed and told us the stories were exaggerated, and anything we ate at that restaurant would be safe.

When we looked around, we were shocked at how extremely generous the servings were. We decided to order one serving of the same thing the legislator chose. We figured we'd take half of it back to the apartment for another day. The food was delicious. Together we couldn't even eat half of the order. The legislator cleaned her plate. Dave paid the bill and started back to the table.

BARRIER FREE?

All of a sudden, Dave's face turned ashen. He said he felt a gurgling sensation. His body let him know he needed to get to the toilet, and fast. When he got to the door of the men's room, he discovered it was occupied. When I saw the look of panic on Dave's face, I excused myself, ran across the restaurant toward the men's restroom door where Dave sat, and grabbed the back of his chair. We raced across the parking lot to our accessible apartment.

I pushed Dave into the bathroom, and went to close the front door. Seconds later Dave yelled to let me know he needed my assistance, now. The toilet and sink were arranged in such a way that he couldn't get close enough to transfer onto the toilet seat. We had never before experienced this situation. The gurgling was getting louder. He was sure he couldn't make the transfer in time. Before he could say anything more, I grabbed the handles at the back of his chair, and spun him around. I jerked his pants off in a second, spun him back around, and pushed the front of his wheelchair next to the front of the toilet. He was panicking, fearing it was too late. Before he could say anything, I grabbed him gently under the arms and lifted him onto the toilet as he started to transfer. He was sitting on the stool, looking at the wall behind the toilet. It was none too soon. He flushed the toilet often. Out of exhaustion from the experience, he leaned his arms on the back of the toilet. A second surge brought him back to a sitting-up position. All of a sudden, my insides gurgled and I knew I was in trouble. I asked Dave how long he would be on the seat. One look in the mirror let me know I had suddenly turned pale as a ghost. Dave said he knew he was going to be there quite awhile. By that time, I felt faint and was holding onto the toilet tank behind the toilet seat. Dave quickly grabbed the wastebasket at his feet, and handed it to me. Fortunately, it had two plastic bags in it. None too soon, I joined him at the wall, and we held hands as we rested our heads on the cool ceramic toilet tank. When the final surge was over, Dave washed off, and I helped him back onto his chair.

While I showered, Dave put on pajamas, and went to bed. I quickly joined him. We slept for nearly eleven hours before the alarm rang, letting us know it was 4:30 a.m., time to get ready to catch the ship AMHS LeConte.

We took a special all-day trip on the ship AMHS LeConte out of Juneau to Pelican, a small community clinging to the side of a mountain. The ship visits these one hundred and fifty people every two weeks to bring supplies and take away frozen fish. Pelican has no roads, only a boardwalk, perhaps a fifth of a mile long. The only vehicles are four-wheel ATV's and a forklift truck.

All of the community's homes are on wood pilings along the boardwalk, with some residents growing produce and flowers in pots suspended between the boardwalk and their homes. There was a handicap accessible ramp leading up to one house. Village residents were so friendly, bringing chairs out on their front stoop to talk to visitors. One woman had built a large hothouse window that extended out about twenty-two or twenty-four inches. She grew tomatoes in the window. Her mouth was salivating as she told us she and her husband were eating their first vine-ripened tomato that evening. She pointed to the one red tomato on the vine. It was a little larger than a grape tomato. She looked so proud.

The store apparently had a good deal on black olives because they had what appeared to be a five-year supply.

We were told the school system is more than adequate. The buildings and equipment are modern. One teacher we talked with said he taught eight students. On board for the return trip was the community's first peace officer. Also on board was the sister of a member of the committee who had interviewed and hired him. She explained the community felt they had the need for a person of authority who could be a good role model because their young people had begun to be rude and they wanted to put a stop to it immediately. Their rudeness was a result of the island buying a TV dish. Local people had never heard such rudeness before, but quickly copied it.

"WHEELCHAIR ACCESSIBILITY"
LOSES ITS ACCESSIBILITY

How pleased we were to travel on the AMHS Kennicott, the pride of the Alaskan fleet. This ship was commissioned in September 1998, and designed to rescue survivors of accidents as well as to help in case of another oil spill. Valdez was a short stop as we headed toward Seward. Nearly everyone left the ship to tour this famous city. All passengers had to be back on board at 8:45 p.m. The ship was to leave promptly at 8:55 p.m. Since the tour bus had no accessible lifts and could not accommodate us, a staff person offered to drive six of us through town to the terminal. The husband of the first couple she dropped off was eighty and used a wheelchair.

David and Anne Davey celebrating Dave's 63rd birthday at Henry's in Alaska.

The other passengers were a middle aged woman and her mother who used a walker. The staff person drove to the terminal to drop off the first couple. She turned the van around, and then dropped four of us off at the famous Totem Inn so we could have dinner. Her last instructions were, "Call the terminal around 8:00 p.m. and we'll send someone to pick you up." At 7:45 p.m., the daughter of the passenger using a walker called to tell them we were ready. We waited about twenty minutes, and then the woman called again. The terminal manager told her she had sent her assistant to the ship to tell them. She assured us they would be there before 8:30 so we would have plenty of time. At 8:30, I called her. She told me the communication system between the terminal and the AMHS Kennicott was not operating. There was nothing more she could do. I informed her that I'd call the police. Our van and everything we owned except for a fifty-dollar American Express Traveler's check was on the AMHS Kennicott. The police station assured us the ship would not sail until we were on board.

I flagged down a policeman, but he said he was on his way to an accident. The clock said 8:50 p.m. We heard the whistle of the AMHS Kennicott blowing several miles away. The other woman and I were trying to flag down any vehicle. One of the large tour buses, taken by many of the ship's passengers, was coming. The clock said 9:02 p.m. We wondered if the ship had left port at 8:55 p.m. The woman got the bus driver's attention, and he pulled into the driveway next to us. A Kennicott passenger that we recognized was in the bus. A friend of hers had left her expensive camera in a bus, and she refused to let her friend leave port without it. It was evident that Dave could not be lifted into that bus. The bus driver spotted a small van returning from the ship. He flagged it down and explained the situation. By this time, it was nearly 9:30 p.m. Before Dave knew how it happened, the two vehicle drivers and the younger woman lifted his chair and him into the small van. The older lady and I climbed in, and the van followed the bus to the AMHS Kennicott. A greeting party met us on the ground while all other passengers and staff members were hanging over the rail watching the bus and van arrive.

The loading dock where Dave entered and exited the ship was closed. A lengthy discussion of the situation followed. It was decided that it was impossible to re-open the ship; it was imperative that we leave port in a few minutes. Therefore, they would lower the large emergency platform for us. This platform was designed to rescue a passenger who might fall overboard, or persons from another ship. We were looking forward to this experience. After about twenty minutes, it became apparent that the lift was not working. Another discussion followed. Plan B was to lift Dave in his chair up the six flights of the outside stairway; his chair was seven inches too wide. After about fifteen or twenty minutes of searching, a small child's wheelchair was produced beside Dave's. He was lifted and poured into the chair. They took him up the first section of stairs and pushed a button. The entire stairway flattened out, even with an upper floor, and Dave was pushed onto the boat amid cheers from the watching audience.

The steps went back down and the older lady, followed by the captain and his assistant, started up the first section of stairs. When the captain pushed the button, nothing happened. After an arduous, tedious climb up the other five flights, she received her applause. Dave told the captain of my fear of heights, and said he was concerned I might pass out. The stairs were once again lowered. The remaining staff members and I followed the captain's assistant up the stairs. My fear of heights was relieved by my desire to leave port. Some men were assisting me from above and others were assuring me from below. While this was happening, Dave was deluged with questions. When Dave made his way to the purser, she told him that the master captain had personally called the Chief of Police to assure him that David Davey and party were aboard the ship, and we were leaving port. When the button was pushed to bring in the steps, nothing happened. It took two staff members and their assistants quite some time to manually pull in the stairway. The cover door to the steps wouldn't close. Experts had been contacted and would be waiting in Seward to fix the problems. We knew this was not going to be a good night.

Because of the lateness of our leaving, the captain did not put down the stabilizers. This allowed him to make up part of our time loss. Our room window was near the deck where many of the passengers were heard and seen losing their dinner during the night.

The next morning as we arrived in Seward, we were told that the ship would not leave port until everything was working. When we looked out of our hotel room window, we noticed the ship sitting in the dock long after its scheduled time of departure.

The Master Captain served as captain of the AMHS Tustumena later when we went to Dutch Harbor, and we became friends. He seemed like a fine Christian man.

MAINLAND ALASKA

We enjoyed several weeks in mainland Alaska. Our fun included a flight from Fairbanks to Barrow with an overnight stay at the Top of the World Hotel. Oil has lifted community and personal economy of this unique native-controlled village to new standards; the community owns its own water treatment plant and sewage system, safety services, grocery store, tourist company, and other businesses. After village expenses, the oil profits are divided among every tribe member.

The school system is outstanding and each native student is encouraged to attend college at the expense of the tribe. A free nursing home is provided for members who need it, as well as free meals to those who are unable to prepare their own.

In the new Culture Center, native children and adults entertained us; they shared their songs and dances. They invited the many tourists to form a circle and hold the rope that is attached to the outside of a large trampoline. The large round trampoline was made from large walrus hides sewn together. A native climbed onto the middle of the skins. On the cry of "three," a quick yank threw the native high into the air. The weight distribution to so many of us gave disillusionment. It felt like we were holding no weight as the native bounced on the skins several times before coming to a stop. It was a memorable experience for Dave and me. Later, women sold items they made from the tribe's kills.

We went on a very detailed tour of the community. The community tour turned around at the DEW Line where the Air Force Base is manned and protected by a limited number of airmen. The entire base still stands ready to defend our country if the need arises. Within hours, the base could be filled with servicemen from other Alaskan bases. The men stationed at this base have to be lonelier than the 'Maytag Repair Man' claims to be.

I walked beside an iceberg in the icy water of the Chukchi Sea, which becomes part of the Arctic Ocean. I also scooped up a Mountain Dew bottle full of the ocean water for Dave to dabble his feet in after it was a little warmer. It was important to me that Dave could also say he put his foot in the Arctic Ocean water. This was a fun trip.

We also enjoyed a special after-hours expedition, via a Hummer, to the northernmost point of land in the Arctic Ocean. There are no paved roads on this strip of land that is comprised of sandy gravel and frozen permafrost. The unique feature of automatically deflating the tires of the Hummer allowed us to glide over the soft gravel.

The extended narrow strip of land separates the Chukchi Sea and the Beaufort Sea, before they join the Arctic Ocean. These two seas wash ashore dead whales, walruses, unique bones, ivory and other collectible items. The scheduled two-hour trip lasted much longer because the young Oriental couple with us desperately wanted to find any fragment of ivory so they had the driver stop often. While the couple searched for ivory, I was taking pictures of the beautiful tiny flowers blooming on the frozen permafrost. The colors were so vibrant, and their shape so perfect. I found a flipper bone of a sea otter. The Oriental couple expressed disappointment that it wasn't their find. Dave had me keep it for our collection. A person is allowed to stay only one night in the village so we departed early the next morning.

We tried to stay at Bed and Breakfasts when they were wheelchair accessible and affordable. The owners were delightful. They brought us enough breakfast to feed at least six people. We ate, then took the fruit and baked goods with us. We often made a peanut butter sandwich and had the remaining breakfast as our main meal. One lovely home near Anchorage was owned by a couple that thought of everything. They had an outside elevator with a roof on it, plus an inside elevator which opened into the large dining room. Their antique table could comfortably seat twenty. The table was over one hundred and fifty years old as were most of their other beautiful antiques. Their antique rectangular grand piano was so heavy it took eight men to carry it in, with the huge legs carried separately.

Dave driving through Denali, Alaska 1999

Dave was one of the lucky people who received a special permit to drive through Denali Park. He applied for it nearly twelve months before we went. We drove about sixty miles into the park. The park ranger warned us that the twenty-five previous days in Denali had been cloudy and the mountain was barely visible. It was cloudy when we started, but the sun was shining as we passed the station and began to spot the large grizzly bears that were in the riverbeds below, or eating berries behind the bushes near the road. Herds of mountain sheep, caribou, foxes, wolves, and flocks of ptarmigans entertained us as we drove along the narrow gravel road that hugs the cliffs, several hundred feet above the rivers and land below. My fear of heights was partially overcome by my desire to get good pictures. On the way into the park, we were beside the mountains so I drove. On the way out, I was on the passenger's side of the van. The tires on the right side of the van appeared to be off the road. My fear quickly returned when I looked straight down. Tours are given in school buses. When two buses are nearing each other, one is expected to stop. The road is just wide enough for them to pass, with less than twenty inches between their mirrors.

Cans of GUNK we carried in our Emergency Kit allowed us to drive the van to have our two flat tires repaired.

The thrill of flying over the park on our way to circle Mt. McKinley that evening in a helicopter was awesome. When we arrived at 'The Mountain', the cloudbank that normally surrounds it was settling in at about eleven thousand feet. The pilot was at eleven thousand, five hundred feet and climbing when Dave noticed that he didn't do well at that height without a pressurized cabin. The view under the cloudbank was fantastic. The pilot quickly brought us down to a lower altitude as we returned to Denali.

REVERSE PSYCHOLOGY

The following day we rode through Denali on one of the school buses. We were the first in line for the bus we would ride. Some boisterous men and women standing two buses down saw us. One of the men, probably in his early 30's, came over and asked if we were riding that bus. Dave told him we were. The man turned on a frown and told Dave that his group had ridden our bus the day before and the driver was awful. He advised us to change buses. With that, he and his group entered their bus and were on their way. I made a suggestion. Within a few minutes, our line formed. Dave and I went down the line telling everyone that we had the best bus driver in the crew and asked everyone to let him know how glad they were that we had drawn him. Dave was loaded first, at the rear of the bus. He told the driver he heard he was the best tour driver in the park. He smiled and said he had worked there for many years so he knew the best areas to stop. I entered the bus next, so I could sit by Dave. I told the driver how grateful I was to be on his bus. He beamed. One by one all the passengers did as we asked them.

The driver was great. He was patient when we had good opportunities for great photos or movies. When we arrived at the other end of Denali and stopped for the normal break, he let our bus passengers take as long as they wanted. Most bus drivers were adamant that they wanted to be back on time, so they expected their passengers to be back on their bus in fifteen minutes. This didn't allow them the time to climb any of the inviting areas that were there. When I looked around, I spotted the man who had warned us about our driver. As he was griping to his friends about them being on the worst bus, his driver ordered everyone into his bus.

At each rest stop, our driver took the time to unload and reload Dave. Riding a bus was an entirely different experience for Dave. The wheelchair tie-downs are located at the back of the bus. He probably spent sixty percent of his time hanging over the cliffs as we rode along. Viewing the animals was a double thrill for him.

A fun-loving singing group in our bus led us in some songs. They asked the driver for his favorite songs. Everyone, including the driver, joined in. Everyone was having a good time. At the end of the ride, everyone complimented the driver on being even better than we were told. Dave and I weren't surprised when he told all of us that we were the best passengers he'd had all summer. He let us know the passengers he had the day before were loud and rude. He said he finally was so frustrated at their immaturity he just quit talking to them, and had considered making this his last year of giving tours. Everyone encouraged him to continue. Of course our bus was the last one back because our people had enjoyed themselves at the other end.

When we left the bus, we went inside the reservations building. Our passengers went up to other tourists and suggested they ask for our driver's bus, and to let him know that we had recommended him. They told them about all the bear pictures we were able to get, and how the driver slowed down while a moose was following the bus. They told the people making reservations how he allowed us to hang out the windows and make videos of the unusual scene. Dave showed them some of the good footage we shot of the moose, bears, foxes, and other animals. By the time we left the building, our driver's bus was fully scheduled for the next day. Dave heard some of the tourists telling the ticket agent they would wait another day to get that driver. That evening, most of the people on our bus ate at the restaurant where the singers were entertaining. A fun evening!

BEAR HIERARCHY

In Homer, everyone urged us to go salmon fishing because the reds (salmon) were in full force in the neighboring rivers. Instead, Dave convinced me to take a six-passenger floatplane into the wild to take pictures of the bears. We were told they flocked to the area where the river looks red because the salmon are so plentiful. Dave watched as the other four passengers, (two of them professional photographers) and I, dressed in waders and warm clothing, followed the pilot to board the small plane. The pilot carried a loaded rifle in case there was a bear problem. We learned that the grizzly (brown) bear normally wouldn't attack unless its young are in danger. We were told black bears not only attack, but also will eat humans like any other animal they kill. The pilot told Dave there were no black bears where he was taking us.

The plane flew over rivers, mountains, an active volcano, lakes, glaciers and thousands of fishermen and women before the plane landed on a small lake near a river. After walking about 20 feet to shore, the six of us walked across the tundra. Each time we came to a deep gully, we had to slide down on the seat of our pants, and then pull ourselves up by holding onto roots of trees and bushes. All this was done with our waders on. We repeated this several times until we were about a mile from the plane. There were holes in the seat of my pants where they had caught on rocks or roots when I slid down the gullies. I left the pants in Alaska. I assured Dave that that part of the trip really wasn't wheelchair accessible.

The pilot left the photographers and me next to the river while he flew two of the passengers, a man and his son from Germany, to a different site. For hours, the photographers and I sat or stood taking pictures and videos of many large grizzlies and two mother bears with twin cubs. I took videos of the two largest bears fighting over the right to stand at a certain spot where the water was red with the salmon jumping and swimming by. The video let Dave see bear hierarchy in action. One large bear situated himself about thirty-five feet below the photographers and me as it jumped and leaped after its choice of the big reds. A flock of sea gulls awaited the leftovers. I took some awesome pictures. The other photographers make their living selling their pictures to sports magazines and calendar companies. My movies turned out great.

I took one hundred rolls of film into a Fred Meyer store in Portland, Oregon to be developed. We were told that all thirty-two rolls that had the bear pictures were lost in the developing department. They were never found. The other sixty-eight rolls were awesome. We chose to have our remaining two hundred rolls developed at Sam's Club in Portage, Michigan when we returned home. No film was lost.

EAGLES AND CROWS

Our van was left at the port in Homer as we set sail for Dutch Harbor in the Aleutians aboard the AMHS Tustumena, the oldest ship of the fleet. The trip to Dutch Harbor has very few passengers because the water is usually rough from the expected fifteen-to-seventeen foot waves. In July, they experienced turbulent water and twenty-nine foot waves. Our August trip was the best the crew could remember. Two to four foot waves and calm water made the trip a real treat for everyone. We were surprised one afternoon when the forest ranger informed us we should look to the mountain on the port side of the ship to see a herd of wild buffaloes that had been brought there several years prior. Stops were made at Kodiak, Port Lions, Chignik, Sand Point, King Cove, False Pass, and Akutan on the way to Dutch Harbor.

Films shown by the forest ranger educated us on Alaska's important role in World War II. We were able to see bunkers that helped protect the United States against Japan when they invaded the Aleutians. We were told that more Japanese soldiers stationed there during WWII committed suicide than on any other assignment. Fortunately, the weather was so bad the year of the invasion that the Japanese refused to stay. I shudder to think what could have happened if the weather had been mild.

The purser on the AMHS Tustumena was driving into Dutch Harbor for gas and to buy newspapers for the crew. Because the tour bus was unable to take Dave into town, the purser invited Dave and me to join her in the ship's wheelchair accessible van. Unfortunately, no freight planes had landed for three days so the papers weren't too current. The driver had a young man to help push Dave's chair across the church yard and into a church. It allowed us to tour the Russian Orthodox Church where local residents worship.

While we were in Dutch Harbor, we were treated to the sight of hundreds of eagles, resting atop every roof and lamppost in town. At the edge of the water, other eagles were feasting on the fish parts left from the cannery. When Dave commented to a local resident on the great number of birds, the resident asked Dave where we lived. The man turned to Dave and, frowning, said, "In Michigan you have your crows, and in Dutch Harbor, we have our eagles." One small plane came in as we headed back to the ship. The gates of the main road closed as the airplane landed on the runway that begins on the road. After the plane passed, the gate opened and we continued our journey. This fishing village of less than two thousand residents, known as Unalaska or Dutch Harbor, exports more fish than any other port in the world.

On the trip back to Homer, as we ate supper in the dining room one sunny evening, whales entertained us off our port side—right at our window, not twenty-five feet from the ship, leaping and falling on their backs into the water. The following afternoon, there was a short shower as we sat at the same table. Within seconds, the sun came out and the largest rainbow we had ever seen joined the mountains on one side of the water to the mountains on the other side.

When we returned to Homer, we were alarmed to notice that we had neglected to lock one of the doors of the van before we left for the week. Nothing was touched, including a considerable amount of cash in the ashtray that was visible from the outside. The ticket clerk had told us that all vehicles left there are safe. She was right.

When we arrived at the Mt. McKinley View Motel, about two-hundred miles from Denali, CNN's big truck was pulling out of the cinder and gravel driveway. The eighty-four-year old owner, Mary Carey, and her daughter, Jean Richardson, are writers. Jean told us CNN had interviewed Mary Carey because of her latest book, an autobiography. She sold movie rights to the book. We were unable to meet Mary, as she had to rush out to catch a plane for Indonesia. When Mary returned to the U.S., she was scheduled to go to Hollywood to serve as a consultant for the film. We enjoyed reading her books but we never have heard if the film was made.

Only in Anchorage and Juneau were there TVs in our rooms. Phones were seldom available. Jean told Dave that Tom Schaberg, Dave's Board president at Goodwill, had left word for Dave to call him as soon as he arrived. When Dave asked where the pay phone was located, Jean laughed aloud, and then told him the nearest pay phone was over an hour's drive. She then explained what a radiophone is. She and seven other businesses share one radiophone line. Dave started to dial Tom when the weatherman came on the line and cut him off. Jean said it can take twenty-to-thirty minutes to get a credit card purchase approved. She told Dave that the party line members had an agreement to limit all calls to five minutes.

She also told him that the other seven people would be listening in on his call so he should be kind in his communication.

Our room was located in an addition at the back of the original hotel. Jean Richardson walked us to our room as night was quickly approaching. The walkway was covered and lit, but not enclosed. Jean stopped to show us a very large open dog's bed at the head of the stairway around the corner from our room. She warned us not to come out of our room if we heard any noise coming from that area. They are sometimes visited by a bear who chooses to sleep in the dog bed. She instructed us to wait until it was light enough for us to see if the bear was gone before coming for breakfast.

SKAGWAY

When we took the highway leading to Skagway, we stopped at a turnout to take pictures of the International Falls. These Falls are quite high. The water cascades down into three sections. At the bottom, half of the water flows into Alaska, while the other half flows into the Yukon in Canada.

A rain cloud literally swooped down on the turnout, and total darkness covered the mountain in seconds. Dave could barely see as he slowly drove down the mountain. After he had descended about four-hundred feet, the sky cleared up in front of the car, but, looking back, we saw only a black cloud wall, and we were unable to see the falls.

Less than a mile before we entered Skagway, I prayed aloud that Dave would be able to see a big bear really close. Within a minute, Dave pulled over to see what a man was taking pictures of when a huge brown grizzly bear appeared within thirty-feet of the van. He acted like a trained bear as he entertained us with his antics. Dave was amazed as we took movies and photos.

As soon as we drove into Skagway, it was obvious that the heart of the city is the train station. Many tracks are available for the narrow-gauge trains that carry passengers to Canada and back.

Some tracks stopped at the docks where we saw the trains fill up with people from the deluxe cruises. Dave made reservations for the following morning trip. The ticket officer told Dave that a special wheelchair accessible car would be on the train leaving at 10:45 a.m. When we arrived, there were several trains on the tracks. The conductor pushed Dave across the tracks and onto the chair lift of the train with the accessible car. Because he caught Dave's wheel in the lift, the tire on the left back wheel of his wheelchair came loose. The conductor and another employee put it back on during the trip.

Nothing could have prepared us for the awesome sights we saw. Everyone was apprehensive about how close the train actually is to the wall of the mountains that hold the track. Many times my elbow would have been removed if it had been out the window. Ivy, hanging from the stone, often hit the window of the train as we swept by at thirty-five miles an hour. A guide described the highlights of what we could expect to see and the history of the area. The sight of the beautiful International Falls was nearly missed when she neglected to alert us of their upcoming presence.

The beauty of rivers, waterfalls, and other scenery across the huge valley impressed us. When we viewed the huge stone that had killed some of the workers on the original track, we realized the dangers they shared. The stone appeared to be about forty feet square, and individual tombstones identify the bodies that are buried under its weight forever. Some famous notorious people occupy another graveyard we passed. The reputation and fame motivated many photographers walking in the graveyard to take pictures of several individual stones.

The guide pointed out entranceways to silver and gold mines on the hills across the canyon. The wooden bridges spanned the deep gorges and added a thrill that couldn't be matched at an amusement park. Some of the gorges ended at a mountain where we passed through dark tunnels into an entirely different scene.

As our guide told us many details, my mind went back in history, wondering how any of the hopeful miners ever survived the Dawson Trail. We passed the trail that everyone had to walk to get to Dawson and other areas where gold was so bountiful. The trail was often no wider than twelve to eighteen inches with a steep drop-off. The guide said that many overloaded animals and miners fell from the path. Not only was there no place for the miners to rest, but there were thousands of people who paid to take that trail every day.

When we arrived at the train's destination in Canada, the engine turned around and went to the back of our train. All the seats were reversed and people were asked to move from their side of the car to give the people who had been on the inside seats a chance to see the ravine side of the view.

We could hardly believe it was the same scenery that we had seen just ninety minutes before. Instead of being at the front of the train, we were now at the back. We watched the train as it made its many curves. We marveled at the sights. Being able to see where you're going can be a little too thrilling.

We could see many patches of rock below the track where it barely clung to the side of the mountains. In many places, it appeared large sheets of steel had been literally drilled and bolted into the rock of the mountain with huge rods. Huge overhead boulders that seemed to be balanced by a small stone made our minds wonder if we would clear that area before the boulder came down. When I looked at the other passengers in our car, I could see a drained expression on their faces. Their eyes were fixed on the same questionable areas that Dave and I viewed. When we finally stopped, the guide said, "And here you are, alive and safe." Everyone in our car said in unison, "Thank God!" It reminded Dave and me of the young voice in Wrangell Narrows, "That was more fun than a roller coaster." Dave and I both were pleased we had come, but agreed that we would never "ride that roller coaster" again.

Aboard the AMHS Columbia on the return trip to Bellingham, Washington, we met many Christians, including the purser and several staff members. Many opportunities arose for us to comfort, minister and witness to lonely and hurting people. Other people came up and told us of their love for Jesus Christ. As we left the ship, many people who came to hug us and kiss us goodbye shared the fact that they had not planned to take that specific trip, but felt the Lord had them change their schedule so they could meet us. It was so wonderful to be used by the Lord.

Wherever we went throughout Alaska, people openly and fully shared their trust in Jesus. Whether Eskimo, Native American, or others who had moved to this beautiful land, they were willing to share their personal trust in Him as their source of eternal life with God. As we held hands and quietly prayed for our food during a meal, people apparently saw us, and would stop next to our table, asking if they could sit down and talk. Some were hurting with tragedies in their own lives; some just wanted to share their love and appreciation for Jesus. They were not ashamed to share the Gospel of Jesus Christ. We appreciated the opportunity to share with them too, reaffirming that this special opportunity in our lives was, indeed, a blessing from God.

Chapter 18

Homeward Bound

AFTER DEPARTING THE AMHS Columbia in Seattle, we spent a day seeing Mt. St. Helens before arriving in Portland, Oregon. What destruction we witnessed at Mt. St. Helens as we looked over miles of blackened forest remains. They had been devastated by the hot ash and blasts that blew trees and mountaintops away as the mountain literally blew its top. We learned that an earthquake had done part of the damage at the time the volcano took its toll. When I returned to the site in 2009, it was interesting to see the mountain was no longer sunken as it was when Dave and I saw it. The forest ranger informed us that the mountain is rebuilding itself.

In Portland, Julie and her partner Stacy took us across the famous bridges, to the Railroad Station, Powell Book Store, Goodwill Industries, City Library, Farmer's Market, famous restaurants, one of the world's largest health food stores, and the Colombian Gorge. What a thrill to get to spend the time with Julie and Stacy. Julie had made arrangements for me to do "The Witness of the Innkeeper" at a nursing home near her apartment. Some of her friends accompanied us there.

IT'S A WIDOW, NO, IT'S A MIRACLE

I am a Christian storyteller and was able to tell "The Witness of the Innkeeper" in several churches, senior centers, and nursing homes in Alaska, Mitchell, South Dakota, and Portland, Oregon. The Alaskan churches in Hope, and Homer, Alaska hosted potluck dinners that allowed us to meet many fine Christians. Other churches in Alaska invited all churches in the city or village to come hear the story.

When we were still in Alaska, I awoke and told Dave that I felt the Lord had told me He wanted me to do "The Witness" in Mitchell, South Dakota. Several times in the weeks ahead, I was awakened with the same feeling. Dave told me that would be impossible because we would arrive there mid-day on Thursday. Our plan was to arrive home on the afternoon of Saturday, September 18th. We prayed a lot for Robert and Sandy Conner, the pastor and his wife in Mitchell, and asked people all along the way to put Robert on their church prayer chains.

One night I was convinced I was to tell "The Witness of the Innkeeper" in Mitchell, and prayed aloud that, if God wanted me to, He would need to work something out because Dave wasn't planning to get me there. Within minutes of my prayer, Dave felt compelled to call his brother Max to see how he was. When Dave finally reached him, Max told Dave that he wanted us to come to their home on Saturday, September 18th. Their grandchildren, Julia and John, were going to be baptized that day. Dave told Max we'd love to come but we wouldn't be home by then. Dave said Max sounded as disappointed as he felt. When Dave hung up, he told me he really wanted to go. Max was going to be sixty-five on the seventeenth and Dave wanted to do something special for him to let him know how much he loved him. I agreed.

Dave had to cancel rooms scheduled for the thirteen nights after we left Portland. The only way to get home in time to rest up and prepare something for Max was to drive considerably more miles per day on the way home. I offered to drive as many miles as Dave felt he could stand to ride. Again I felt I needed to tell "The Witness of the Innkeeper" in Mitchell. There were no rooms available in or near Mitchell because of a large wedding that weekend. The closest room Dave could get reservations for Saturday night was 75 miles from Robert's church. I told the Lord I agreed to leave it in His hands.

Saturday night in South Dakota provided the most frightening night of the trip. We had just arrived at our motel when Dave noticed a huge black spider on the wall. It was behind a lamp on my bedside stand, and it was impossible for Dave to reach it with a shoe. I was unloading the van, so Dave called me to see if I could reach it. About the only things I'm afraid of are heights and spiders. I couldn't reach the spider, and felt it was a black widow. The motel clerk arrived with a very long-handled fly swatter and, after three swats, killed it. She announced there are lots of black widow spiders in that area. However, she said she had smashed it so badly she couldn't identify it. It should have alerted us when the employee told us to not worry if we had to kill anything on the walls because they had a special paint that was washable.

I sprayed the carpet and baseboard around the entire room with a can of spider spray we carried on the trip in the van. We left the light on all night. I awoke during the night with the hair on my arms standing up. Using Dave's shoe, I had to stand on the bed to kill the twin just above Dave's head. When I looked around, I was horrified to see that the rest of the family invaded the wall and ceiling. After annihilation of the invaders I could reach, I used the can's contents around the entire ceiling. The walls were covered with the legs and other body parts I left as I proceeded to annihilate the next victim.

At 4:30 or 5:00 a.m. on Sunday morning, Dave awoke with a start. I was sitting up in bed, visibly shaken. Dave thought it was the sun that filled our room with a brilliance we have never before or since experienced. Dave asked me to turn off the lights and to close the drapes. I turned off the overhead light. I told Dave the lights were off and the drapes hadn't been opened. When I opened and closed the drapes, it was still dark outside. Dave and I felt like Saul on the road to Damascus. The brilliant light suddenly disappeared, and the room was in total darkness. I quickly switched on the lights. When Dave looked around the room and saw the remains of the spiders on the wall, he said he knew God was telling him that I was going to do the "Witness of the Innkeeper" in Mitchell. He counted fifty-four upside-down bodies of the black spiders lying on the carpet, plus the trophies on the wall. A few minutes later, I called the motel clerk. She identified the bodies as Black Widows.

We dressed, packed up, and drove to Mitchell. We couldn't remember the location of the church. I prayed that, if God wanted us to go to church at Calvary, He would have to find the church for us. Immediately, I remembered that Sandy had written their new home address in the journal we kept. We looked up the address and drove there. I was concerned if Robert was still alive, but Dave reminded me that God had told him Robert would not die in 1999. I nodded and went to the door to ask if he was there or at the church. His teenage daughter said he was coming downstairs. When Robert came outside, we could see he wasn't well. He told us he experienced an asthma attack during his chemotherapy treatment on Thursday. He was so cold he wore his winter coat and gloves although it was very warm. When we hugged him, he seemed so frail.

I told Robert I had done "The Witness of the Innkeeper" several times in Alaska and Oregon. When I asked him if he would like me to do it that morning at his church, he gladly accepted my offer. He said he was pleased that he could rest and save his message for the following Sunday.

After the service, a couple hugged me and told me they were from West Virginia. The woman said she and her husband had attended a large wedding the previous evening at another church, and were lost on their way there this morning. When they came around the corner and spotted Calvary Baptist, she told her husband that she felt they should attend service there. When I was telling the story, the woman said she and her husband squeezed hands and looked at each other. They knew that God had sent them there to hear the story. She said they had attended a church for thirty years and had never heard the story of Christ preached.

Later at the restaurant, Dave told Robert it was great how God works. He said we were there early because we were going to his brother Max's home for the baptism. Robert's response came with a smile, "Yes, it is great how God works, but that isn't why you are here today, Dave. God sent you here because I needed you. I prayed you'd make it back so Anne could give today's message. I was upstairs expecting you when Anne rang the doorbell."

Robert died in January 2000. We thanked God that He gave us the opportunity to know Robert and his wife Sandy. God showed us time after time that this trip wasn't just to see beautiful sights. He had a plan for us everywhere we went.

Chapter 19

Max's Day

ALL THE WAY home from Alaska, we hurried as much as we could. Dave had his laptop computer with him, so he decided to write a message to read to his brother Max. He wanted to remind Max of how proud he always was to be his brother. When we got back to Portage, we ordered a huge birthday cake. I drove all over town, gathering items to have the cake decorated properly. A friend of Susan, our daughter, agreed to decorate it. I found very small blue and pink baby bassinettes to designate the birth of Max, Margaret, Diane, Julia and John. I also found little figurines to designate graduation, weddings, and other significant times. Dave traced quarters on black poster board and cut them out. He put the title of two of Max's records on them, and put them on the cake at the appropriate place. In the meantime, Dave spent two or three days selecting pictures of Max and the family, and gluing them onto poster boards as a gift to Max. The pictures included covers from two of Max's records. One was with Pat Boone and the other with Sherri Lewis.

Max's family and friends at Max and Margaret's home

When we arrived at Max and Margaret's, there were many guests. Some were leaders from the church, others were from the choir he directed; and the rest were family and friends. Max took Dave and others for a ride on the pontoon boat. Julia and Jon were baptized in the lake behind Max and Margaret's lovely home.

Jon, Julia, Chip & Diane after baptism at Max & Margaret's Sept. 1999

Jon, Julie, Chip and Diane Dusseau in Max and Margret's back yard, after Julia and Jon were baptized.

After dinner, Dave read the following to Max:

"Happy 65th birthday dear Max! Today we came together to witness the Christian baptism of Julia and John. This has truly been a blessing as they have been faithful to Christ's command. We would not be here today if another birth that was celebrated yesterday had not occurred sixty-five years ago. My dear brother Max was born.

"Max has always been a very special person in my life. In fact, he has been to most of us here. We were born only twenty-three months apart. He is the oldest. He has a great sense of humor and is very sensitive to the feelings of others. Even though Mom said we used to fight like cats and dogs, I always wanted to be like Max.

Max and David Davey celebrate Max's 65th birthday.

"As well as age, he has all the talent, good looks, and an extra eight inches in height. As a kid, I followed him wherever he and his friends went. I'm sure they were sick and tired of me.

"One day when Max was ten or twelve, he was riding over to a friend's house on his new, knee-action, Schwinn bike. I dogged him on my old Western Flyer. I didn't know who he was going to see, I just wanted to be wherever he was. It turned out to be a long way from home. I recall we were riding on Outer Drive when I got a flat tire. Rather than leaving me like many brothers would have, he took me to a gas station and, with his last quarter, paid to have my tire fixed. Then he took me home instead of abandoning me like he could have.

"When we were kids, we roomed together. In those days it wasn't like today when everyone thinks they need their own room. I remember when Max got an old box guitar with only four strings, he'd lie there in bed and play music. He'd say, 'Listen to this.' It was great!

"Also, one time we went out to Walled Lake to the McVey's cottage—people that Mom and Dad knew. Everyone was swimming, fishing or out in the rowboat. Max found an old abandoned violin in an unused bedroom, cleaned it, tuned it, and practiced until he could play a song. He'd never held a violin before.

"Being able to do things without much or any training was not unusual for Max. The way I heard this story was that, while visiting a contractor-friend one day, he tried out operating his back-hoe which takes a great deal of coordination. With only a few tries, Max was able to successfully dig a trench. He could just do it.

"It always amazed Mom the way Max understood music. She often told about one time when she was out with Max. He heard a small cement mixer—the kind that ran on a 2-cycle engine. She would proudly tell how he said, 'Listen Mom, that's a syncopated rhythm.'

"When we were out at Grandpa and Grandma Heaton's farm in Chelsea, the two of us were always climbing up in the haymow, swinging on the rope from one side of the barn to the other. As if that wasn't dangerous enough, we'd throw down a few pitchforks full of hay and jump down to the wood floor below which was loaded with tools, equipment, nails and boards. We thought we were safe.

We would also lie on the grass by the old milk house and watch the birds circle overhead. We thought they were buzzards—or at least I did—and wondered if we lay too still, would they come down to get us.

"Sometimes we would hook up two saw horses to the wheelbarrow with remnants of harness that we found in the shed and would travel for miles in our minds—across country, setting up camp, eating our grub (which Grandma had fixed for us), unhooking the horses, putting them out to pasture, unloading our covered wagon, all in the scorching sun, in the heat of the day. There was often a discussion as to who was in charge of the expedition. Max usually won.

"At night, Grandma would strip us down, stand us up in the cement stationary tubs—one in each tub—to scrub off the residue of the barnyard and the dusty sweat of our journeys. Until our scrub down, we weren't even allowed to go into the bathroom because we were so filthy.

"Grandma was so proud of Max. She would arrange for him to play his horn for the residents of the Chelsea Old People's Home while she accompanied him on the piano.

"Max played in the Cooley High School band and orchestra. I was proud each time I saw him on stage, playing his horn. He looked great, and he sounded great.

"When Max and I were both attending Wayne State University, he played in the marching band which included playing at football games. I still remember one time when he had to play before and during one of their games. He took me over to the stadium because I didn't have any transportation. This made him late so, after we got parked, he loaded his horn on my lap, tipped me back on my big wheels and raced me around the cindered racetrack so he could join the band before they got started. I don't remember anything about the game, but we had a good time. Max enjoys life and always finds fun in what he's doing.

"I always thought Max's old Dodge Coupe was beautiful. It was a great looking car and I think he liked it too. He drove it all over, everywhere, even down to Ohio to buy his fireworks, unknown to Mom and Dad. Whatever happened to those fireworks, Max?

"After Max and Margaret were married, they would include me in some of their activities. This wasn't always easy. They lived upstairs in a flat. I remember Max carried me on his back up that long, narrow stairway just so I could join him and Margaret for one of her delicious dinners.

"In Max's early days as a Christian musician, Margaret, who is an accomplished pianist, accompanied Max and other horn players around the city. We're all aware of the magnificent concerts by the Max Davey Singers with professional and semi-professional musicians, often featuring vocal stars such as those appearing on two of his albums that are on the poster boards we made up for his sixty-fifth birthday.

"Mom was sure proud of Max and his wonderful concerts. She always called and told us about the concerts she or church members were able to attend. One day when she called, she was crying. It seems that Max had introduced her at the concert. Between tears, she told us, 'I am so proud of that boy that sometimes I feel like my heart will burst.'

"Again and again, Max, you have taken mostly untrained voices and built great church choirs through your own enthusiasm, patience and encouragement. You'll never know in this life how many people have been blessed by your willingness to use your God-given talent.

"A good example of your thoughtfulness and generosity was the time all the family got together at the Oakland Mall on the busiest day of the year, December 26th, for a steak dinner. Max, you generously gave silver dollars and large ballpoint pens to all the nieces and nephews. Our David was sharing that event with his children, Lucy and Philip, when he showed them the large pen.

"Father Flanagan had a saying, 'He ain't heavy, he's my brother,' which has a special meaning for me. You made it possible for me to do things and go places like everyone else. This made a great impact of how I've viewed life.

"You're a very special man, Max—one God has had His hand on all these years. No matter which way you have turned, you've known He had a definite plan for your life. You belong to Him.

"Max, we've all been blessed by your years on this earth. Because of the saving grace of Jesus, we will get to enjoy you with Him, forever. But I think I've made an awful mistake for all these years and I want to correct it. I picked up the habit, like many of us do, of not telling you how much you have meant to me and still do. It wasn't on purpose. We sometimes think others somehow automatically understand how we feel about them, and we'll even tell someone else. We really need to tell each other personally, often, maybe every day.

"I want you to know how much I respect, admire and love you. It's not because of what you do, such as your music which I do truly enjoy, but for who you are, my loving, caring, sensitive, humorous brother I always wanted to be like. "Happy Birthday, dear Max! I love you.

"Max, at my birthday party, you sang Ray Boltz's "Thank you." I'd like to read the words to that song right now. It may take me awhile." While Dave read it, tears filled Max's and Dave's eyes much of the time. While glancing around the large crowd of well wishers, I noticed that most eyes were wet during parts of the story.

After dinner, Julia called Jon over and excitedly told him to look at the two bassinettes that had their names and dates of birth under them. She said, "Look Jon. We're part of Grandpa's life." Max smiled as he witnessed her excitement. Julia's friend told her, "When your grandpa was young, I think he looked like Elvis." Max beamed.

(Dave died on July 7, 2005. Max died on December 6, 2007. At Max's funeral, Margaret said she knew Max and Dave would spend Christmas together for the first time in many years.)

Chapter 20

Mackinac Island Memories

ON THE SPUR of the moment in 1989, we decided to visit Mackinac Island for a few days. We had just come from a Michigan Association of Rehabilitation Facilities meeting so we were quite close to the island. The Grand Hotel had no vacancies but recommended we call the Iroquois Hotel. When I called, the Iroquois Hotel owner explained that the wheelchair access to the hotel was through their dining room. Their dining room would open in a week. Although there were steps leading up to the front porch, she considered one guest room on the first floor to be wheelchair accessible, and assured me that bringing Dave up into the lobby was not a problem. She promised the manpower to lift him anytime we wanted to come and go. The owner also told me that her maiden name had been Davey and we were the first Davey family to stay in their hotel. Many times during our stay we were gifted with homemade chocolate chip cookies or brownies.

The room was wheelchair accessible, newly redecorated, and quite beautiful. The layout of the bedroom allowed us to watch the boats and ships as they were passing the island. Wide-open windows, combined with the roofline outside our room, allowed us to be lulled to sleep by the sound of waves and occasional clippity clop, clippity clop of the horses' hoofs as they came down the beautiful street, headed for the Grand Hotel.

As soon as we arrived, we met a young college student whose aunt lived on the island year-round and owned a business. When Dave asked him if he knew anyone who would push him around the island, he was quick to apply for the job. We put a piece of luggage on Dave's feet, and I pulled the larger bags as we went to the lovely Iroquois Hotel. After we had registered and deposited our luggage, the young man gave us a tour of the Grand Hotel. There normally is a charge for entering the Grand Hotel, but they recognized our guide as a resident. He showed us the Fort, and took us on a tour of many sites.

Once I was asleep, the stillness of the room allowed Dave to hear different sounds of the night. He'd awaken me as his ear picked up the sound of an approaching ship coming across the water. How we enjoyed listening to the distant low moaning wail of the ship's horn, sounding both forlorn, and so far away. Dave would tell me periodically, "Now listen Annie." He had it timed perfectly. Sure enough, the sound got louder as the distance shortened. By the fifth blast, we knew it would be only minutes before the freighter, with engines silent, and dimmed lights that exposed her presence in the darkness, would glide through the channel outside the hotel. We held hands as we sat up in bed, awed by the experience we shared. It wouldn't be long before the lights disappeared and we were aware the ship had cleared the island. We listened until we heard the fifth and final faded moan before we drifted off to sleep.

The next morning Dave and I went for a walk to see what happened downtown before tourism became official on Memorial Day. We loved the fact that no private motorized vehicles are allowed on the tourist side of this paradise.

Dave took some great photos of men in coonskin hats and jackets. The men told him that they had personally trapped and tanned the hides on the island.

There was a temporary serenity and calmness on the island we had never witnessed on previous trips. The island seemed like a different place, without the echoes of laughter and chatter of the thousands of tourists that usually fill the streets and sidewalks. Clomp, clomp of the many horses taking tourists to and fro was only an occasional occurrence during our stay.

While storeowners were busily filling their stores with new merchandise, I was trying to talk Dave into going for a ride on one of the buggies or taxis the next day. I pointed to a fine carriage that looked like something Cinderella would have taken to the Prince's ball. Two older ladies were just starting to enter the carriage. I suggested we should ask the driver if Dave would be able to use it. Dave let me know he appreciated life and limb more than the sights, but reminded me that our young guide had given him his phone number. As the ladies were climbing aboard the taxi, our eyes were drawn to the other side of the street. Empty boxes, upon boxes, were sitting in front of a store that had just put their 'Open' sign in the window. A team of large draft horses, pulling a large wagon, stopped in front of the store.

It never was determined what spooked the team of draft horses pulling the large wagon. We were staring at the mountain of empty boxes that were on the wagon, when the man standing below threw several more up to the man who was straddling the mountain. Suddenly the horses bolted! The receiver flew into the air and across the boxes while the draft horses turned to their right and knocked over the two beautiful horses that were waiting to pull the lovely taxi. I felt bad for the ladies and the horses, but I was so grateful it wasn't Dave and me getting in that taxi. The draft horses suddenly decided to make an illegal U turn.

My adrenaline began flowing as the team of horses headed toward Dave and me. I didn't have time to assess in which direction to take Dave. Dave was shocked speechless as well. I thought we should go across the street to get out of harm's way, but when I saw the horses coming, I didn't know which way to turn. Not knowing if they would be on the side of the street I wanted to go, I lifted

Dave's chair up a step and pushed his chair into a recessed storefront. I hoped the high curb and step might discourage the horses from coming in our direction. If they chose to, the area would have offered us no protection against two huge workhorses. They were stopped a few feet in front of us. I pulled Dave's chair down and spun it around so he could view the sad scene. Veterinarians were already checking the two beautiful taxi horses that were still on the ground, whinnying in such a pitiful moan. We heard the next day the horses were going to be fine, but no one in town was sure if the two ladies would ever get over the shock. I never asked Dave to go for a ride during that trip.

OUR LAST TRIP TO MACKINAC ISLAND—1996

As we swiftly flew across the rough waters, the hovercraft turned sharply, allowing the beauty of a full panoramic view of Mackinac Island. Not quite four, our granddaughter Maegan, who had been watching the splashing waters, jumped up and down, squealing with delight, "Look at that big white building! Mommy, Daddy, what is that big white building?"

Dave and I were there with James, Susan, Maegan, and Jessica to celebrate Dave's sixtieth birthday. Finally, we were getting a chance to stay at the famous Grand Hotel on Mackinac Island, Michigan.

The sweet little inquisitive voice demanded, "Grandpa and Grandma, what is that big white house?" Maegan and Jessica were each holding one of Dave's knees waiting for an answer. He started to answer her when Sue and James explained the white building was the Grand Hotel where we were going to be staying. The girls started jumping up and down on the floor with excitement.

As the craft approached the island, the buildings seemed to zoom toward us. We touched the dock, and the craft was tied. Dave's eyes scanned the area for the newest addition to the island, a covered surrey with a wheelchair lift attached to the back. The driver of that surrey was scheduled to meet us there. What a feeling of grandeur we shared when we arrived at the Grand. Their employees made each of us feel very special. The formal doorman helped Sue, James, Maegan and Jessica off the surrey, and onto the famous porch that is the length of a football field.

Because of the steps leading up to the porch, Dave and I entered the first floor to use the elevator. To our amazement, when Dave registered and asked for a room near Sue and James, the manager generously gave us the President's Suite. He told us it was barrier free.

Unlike breakfast and dinner, lunch did not come with the cost of the room. I had ordered lunch for both days when making reservations. This eliminated our having to find a restaurant on the mainland. We cherished every moment on the island. We planned to arrive early, register at the hotel, and have lunch before our rooms would be prepared. We were at the table when Sue and James returned to announce that their room was wonderful. They still didn't know they were staying in the President's Suite.

Susan Gibson holding Jessica, Maegan, Dave and Anne Davey in President's Suite of Grand Hotel, Mackinac Island, MI

After lunch, we went upstairs. The suite consists of a large living room, where the children could run and have fun, between two large bedrooms. Each bedroom had a private entrance so we could come and go without disturbing each other. With the exception of different wallpaper, the bedrooms were similar. Each had two king size canopy beds with two steps which allowed guests to enter their high old-fashioned comfort of luxury. The mattress top was about level with Dave's head as he sat in his wheelchair, admiring the beauty, but feeling like a barefoot mountain climber about to embark up a steep cliff.

The opportunity to stay in the President's Suite isn't offered to everyone. We appreciated that opportunity. The bed situation had to be solved. This was such a huge room that I decided to take the mattress and springs off one bed and simply put them on part of the space at the foot of the bed. If I needed more height, the other bed was there to supply our need. We laughed as we realized that, on the floor, the mattress and springs were nearly the same height as our bed at home.

As we were investigating the living room, we discovered that we also were privileged to have a veranda off the living room. We could sit out there and watch horses and carriages arrive with hotel guests. It was so relaxing. It was the first time we noticed that the roof of the huge porch covered three of these verandas. When Susan was changing Jessica's diaper, I wondered how many rich and famous mothers had also lovingly changed their babies there. None of the guests who were relaxing on the porch below were aware that there were people sitting above them.

In our bedroom, the look of alarm and disappointment on James' face filled the room like a black cloud. He noticed that the bathroom doorway might also be a problem. Sure enough, the doorway was wide enough but the door wouldn't swing in far enough to let Dave clear it. Dave and I smiled at each other. We were told this was a wheelchair accessible suite and we planned to prove them right. There on the small refrigerator sat a knife, presumably for the cheese and fruit inside. Undaunted by the situation, I lifted the pins from the hinges of the door. James and I placed the door against a wall of the huge bathroom. Dave glided easily into the bathroom, and we realized all was not lost. Maegan and Jessica jumped up and down to show their appreciation of the situation.

Somehow the room had taken on a look of uniqueness, almost like it felt smug at throwing off some of its elegance, in favor of being "barrier free." The bed on the floor was remade and we left to see the island. Dave had hired the wagon with a lift to drive us around the island. Before we left, we put the "DO NOT DISTURB" sign on our bedroom door.

As we rode around the island, we saw the unique gift shops and famous Mackinac Island fudge store fronts, always looking like they just had a fresh coat of whitewash. Majestic lakefront homes, and others nestled among the rolling land of the island, serve as a reminder of the past. Rich people used those homes as a summer hideaway. Many of their descendents still enjoy those treasures. How easy it is, in this setting, to leave your problems and obligations of the world of work.

As we rode on the surrey, a man who stood next to the driver took us back in time, with stories of the history of the island. My mind began picturing the splendor of the clothing worn by the passengers departing from the boats many years ago. Dave was thinking back too. He smiled and said, "Perhaps a beautiful clipper ship, with its magnificent white sails, furled to the spar to prevent the wind from claiming the craft once more to the open sea, was their transportation." The man's description allowed my mind to see yards of material in the dresses that went swooping along. Dave wondered aloud if the streets were paved back then. I'm sure there must have been Indians as well as traders and soldiers on those same boats. I could almost picture the first guests of the Grand Hotel, stepping onto the dock. I'm sure the men looked dapper as they came dressed in their handsome suit coats and matching knickers, ready for a game of lawn croquet or badminton. The children probably wore puffy pantaloons and carried their sand buckets and shovels.

My mind could picture the Indians living on the island. When the man told of the different battles that occurred during the time Fort Mackinac was occupied, our minds could clearly picture the scenes his words were painting.

The wagon was made much heavier by the weight of the lift. The extra weight often made it necessary for the driver to use the brakes to prevent the wagon from damaging the horses' hind legs as we went down the steep hills. The horses that pulled this surrey were Belgian draft horses, much heavier than those pulling the beautiful taxis that transported most guests to the Grand Hotel. The large horses galloped past hundreds of lovely hollyhocks that lined the trail. The military graveyard held the graves of several famous people, including that of Governor Milliken.

As we rounded the last hilly curve past the Fort, the wagon jerked as the galloping horses took us past the chapel and stopped at the Grand Hotel.

After the ride, we dressed and met for dinner in the Grand Hotel dining room Men are required to wear a suit, or jacket, and tie; and women are expected to wear dressy clothes. It is interesting how elegant you feel in that dining room. Even Maegan and Jessica seemed to be enveloped in an aura of grandeur.

Maegan leaned over and told Dave, "Grandpa, I feel elegant. Do I look elegant?" He assured her she did, indeed.

"Yes Maegan, you look elegant."

Never were there better-behaved girls of two and four. The dining room photographer captured that feeling of royalty shared by everyone in the dining room. We felt compelled to buy pictures of the family.

After dinner, Dave and I went up to our suite and sat on the veranda. As soon as Dave looked out toward the little lighthouse island, he saw a moose swimming in that direction. It climbed onto the small island, and shook the water off its body.

Dusk had quickly replaced the sunset, bringing the silhouette of the Mackinac Bridge with its lights into full view. The soft city streetlights and carefully placed lighting on the Grand Hotel lawn transformed the island into a romantic getaway for Dave and me. We sat holding hands without saying a word, soaking up the beauty of the moment. It was easy to see why the Governor of Michigan would choose this location for rest and relaxation. One by one, we pointed out scenes that we wanted to share with each other. It nearly took our breath away, and sometimes the beauty made us shed some tears of joy that God had blessed us with this opportunity.

Laughter filled the living room as Sue and James came out to show us the nice goodies that had been left on their pillows when the maid turned down their blankets. No red and white peppermints there. They were laughing as they asked if the blankets on our bed had been turned down. We took the "Do Not Disturb" sign off the ornate doorknob, and went into our room. Yes, indeed. The blankets had been turned down and our bag of goodies was on Dave's pillow. Now, that's class!

When Dave was sitting on the toilet stool, looking out the window at the people sitting on the porch below, a thought occurred to him. If he could sit and hear their conversations, and see the smiles on their faces, how many people down there could see and hear him. I went down to the porch to check it out. I couldn't see or hear a thing in our suite.

As we lay on the comfortable bed on the floor, we enjoyed the clippity clop of the horses on the winding street, as they delivered their last tolls for the evening. The low murmur of voices on the

Grand porch beneath our window relaxed us as we snuggled closer, and shared the time together.

Our plan was to eat an early breakfast and as late a lunch as possible, to get out of our room by the deadline. We needed to go into Canada because we were riding the Agawa Canyon train the following morning.

Before Dave and I went downstairs for breakfast, our suitcases were put out in our foyer. After breakfast, we came back upstairs and went out on the veranda. We wanted one last look before I put the bedroom back into its original order.

We had just gotten on the veranda when the maid came into the suite. She was unaware that we were still there. She went into our bedroom and became very upset. She picked up the phone and was telling someone about the bed and door. She ran out of the room.

Anne Davey and Susan Gibson replace mattress and springs on the bed in the President's Suite of Grand Hotel, Mackinac Island, Michigan

Susan and James came in at that time. Susan and I put the bed back together. After James helped me replace the bathroom door, Susan and James left to go to the dining room with their daughters. As Dave and I looked at the room, it had lost some of its independent flair. Dave couldn't believe the difference. It was a beautiful room, but now it was just a room.

We went back out on the veranda for the last twenty minutes before we had to vacate the suite. Susan and James had barely gone when we heard the woman return to the suite, accompanied by a man. She was almost hysterical, as she described the way we had ruined the room. As they entered our bedroom, the man's voice was stern as he asked her what she was talking about. While they were in the bathroom, with the maid hysterically insisting she knew what she had seen in the room, Dave and I decided to quietly exit. Lunch was waiting.

Chapter 21

Victorian Bed & Breakfast

$\mathcal{W}$E DROVE PAST the front of the lovely old Victorian Bed & Breakfast, and followed the driveway to the rear of the house to park. Immediately we recognized the house as photographed. It was the back of the house that was pictured in newspapers, magazines and on TV. The front of the house that faces the street was rather plain. Although it was a delightful well-kept Victorian house, the outside beauty was truly in the Victorian trim, large porches on both sides of the century old house, and stairways with many steep steps leading up to those porches.

The gardens were beginning to reflect signs of autumn's arrival in Michigan. The summer flowers surrounding the birdbath showed signs of surrender to the first frost, but evidence remained of the blaze of color that had costumed the gardens just days prior to our visit. Flowers seen in most Michigan gardens in October still lent color to the grounds.

As we looked up at the ten or more steps, a little doubt began to creep into our enthusiasm. Our eyes were still searching for a ramp to enter the first floor of the Carriage House where our suite would consume the first floor. The top floor had two Sherlock Holmes bedrooms. Friends of ours, Denny and Kathy Young, were staying in the upstairs bedroom that was over our sitting room. Denny met us at the van to share his observations. First, he was sure Dave couldn't enter, let alone occupy, the suite that we had been dreaming about for nearly fourteen months. Second, there was no elevator, ramp, etc. into the main Inn.

When Dave's eyes met mine, disappointment was mixed with determination. When we first read about the Inn, we both had said, "We have to go there!" Dave had called the very next day. "No," he was told, "the Bed & Breakfast didn't have barrier free rooms yet, but next year it would! The carriage house would have a barrier free suite on the first floor." We could hardly wait. We started saving for a fun evening there.

After a TV show featured the Inn with its unique cuisine, our mouths were salivating every time we talked about our planned night there. It was nearly fourteen months since Dave made the reservations. He had confirmed them six months prior to our date of arrival. He planned it as a joint celebration of our anniversary and my birthday. An acquaintance had told Dave about their great accommodations in the Inn, and how scrumptious the buffalo and pheasant under glass were. The anticipation was as great as the event was going to be. Could we force ourselves to wait another year after hearing that? It wasn't easy.

Dave asked Denny to tell the owner we had arrived and were waiting for him at the bottom of the steps. Dave suggested he would need to provide another able-bodied man to assist in lifting him up the two steps to the porch of the Carriage House, then to the dining room. The owner and a chef apprentice appeared to serve as the musclemen. As Denny and Kathy gave us the guided tour over the one-hundred-plus year old floorboards of the carriage house, Denny pointed out the bathroom. Dave and I started laughing so hard the owner was angry as the tears poured from our eyes. Ah yes! Indeed, a barrier free bathroom! Kathy noted the twelve-inch step-up might be a little hard for Dave to maneuver, to say nothing of the configuration of the room. Trying to control his laughter,

Dave asked me if I could lift him up into the room. After I had successfully pushed him into the tight space, Dave's eyes danced. He pointed out he could wash his face and hands on the left and could safely fit onto the stool, as dubious as the situation appeared to others. We ignored the shower hidden in the wall. I felt it had to be modeled after the one in "Psycho".

I easily took Dave safely down from the bathroom. When we turned around to the lovely old brass bed with its share of white lace and ruffles sitting atop the bed, we noticed it required steps to enter, Dave's eyes met mine as he asked if I felt up to getting him onto that bed. Feeling giddy and adventurous, I said, "Why not?" The two men carried the brass steps to my side of the bed, and then moved the heavy bed over so Dave would have some room to get in. Our friends looked at us in disbelief at our decision to stay.

Then the fun! Dinner! The chef and his apprentice carried Dave down from the porch, pushed him around to the dining room entrance, and probably gave themselves a hernia as they carried him up the flight of steps that seemed endless. The house was appropriately furnished, the dining room was probably set up like a rooming house dining room would have been one-hundred years ago, and we enjoyed looking around in the areas available to the guests. The menu choices were different than we had ever experienced. Dave ordered quail; I ordered elk. It was the first time we had eaten either. Everything was delicious. We later had an opportunity to meet some of the other guests.

Hernia revisited! After cooking the feast for all their guests, the chef and his assistant were again blessed. They had the privilege of carrying Dave carefully down those steps, pushing him along the dirt path, and lifting him onto the porch of the carriage house.

The owner reiterated several times during the evening that he had made the house into a Bed and Breakfast before barrier-free laws went into effect. We knew the truth. I accused Dave of thinking of his own safety in getting up and down steps. He neglected to inform the man that he had been on the Michigan Architectural Barrier Committee that wrote those laws that went into effect three years before the man bought the house. Since they changed the house from residential to serving food as well as an Inn, the code would have affected both buildings. To meet code, a business had to have a ramp that has twelve inches for every inch the building is above the ground. The porch looked like it was at least sixty inches off the ground. Dave didn't have the heart to ruin the man's weekend. He couldn't picture the grounds of the lovely Victorian if they had a fifty-to-sixty-foot ramp in the garden leading up to the house, and a twenty-foot ramp in the parking lot to meet the code for the converted carriage house.

David Davey in sitting room of Bed and Breakfast

Denny and Kathy came to visit us in the suite after dinner. We laughed and talked for about an hour. The parlor had a rattan chaise lounge and chair that gave us ample sitting room. Kathy described the upstairs as two identical bedrooms and a foyer decorated with a Sherlock Holmes theme. They were staying in the bedroom immediately over the parlor. The room next to theirs was situated directly over our bedroom.

After they went up to their Sherlock Holmes room, we got ready for bed. Romantic plans for the evening had been discussed for months. We both got the giggles as Dave was in the bathroom, praising the management for making it so barrier-free. I could hardly help Dave down the twelve-inch step. By the time we were ready for bed, we were weak from laughter.

As Dave struggled to get a good grip on the sheets to assist in getting him onto the bed, we started laughing again. Dave had to sit back and hold the arms of his wheelchair so he could compose himself. This was no easy matter. Finally, after we had spent two or three hours in our attempt, Dave plopped himself into the soft featherbed mattress. I joined Him, and we enjoyed lying there embracing each other for a minute. When Dave mentioned his shoulder and arm were a little sore from clutching the sheet so tightly, the laughter resumed. Dave made hilarious remarks as I rubbed aloe vera lotion on his shoulders and arms. The laughter caused me to need to go to the potty. Since we were completely exhausted from the laughter, it was no surprise when I returned in two minutes, and Dave was unaware that sleep had replaced the amorous night we had planned. I snuggled up next to him and promptly fell asleep as well.

The next morning, I suggested that Dave relax, while I would bring a nice tray of breakfast for us to eat in bed. When I went up to the dining room, the chef's assistant grimaced as he told me that he and the chef were trying to recover from the previous night's weightlifting experience. When I asked him if I could take breakfast in bed to Dave, he was so delighted he carried Dave's tray to him, while I took mine.

After we ate the food, we started to reminisce about the night before and started laughing again. Every time our eyes met, we went into a rage of laughter that left us both weak. This was so unlike our normal behavior. I don't remember any other time that we couldn't stop laughing like we did at that bed and breakfast.

After Dave was safely back onto his wheelchair and into the bathroom, I started to load the van. Before my last trip to the van, I helped Dave come back down into the bedroom.

As I returned from carrying out the last of our belongings, I opened the front door. The occupants of the other Sherlock Holmes bedroom were coming down the stairs. I immediately recognized them as a young couple from Chicago whom we met the previous night in the dining room. They weren't very friendly as I smiled and spoke to them on my way into our suite. When I mentioned what a beautiful day it was, the woman barely nodded. As they were exiting the outside door, the woman turned around and whispered to her husband loud enough that I couldn't miss hearing, "She must be that sex maniac!" When I told Dave a moment later, his eyes twinkled as he sadly commented, "If they only knew!" Of course we laughed so hard I could hardly take Dave down the two steps at the front of the porch.

Chapter 22

Yes, Men In Wheelchairs Have A Sex Life

(DAVE ASKED ME to include this chapter, which he wrote shortly after his retirement in 2000.)

I have asked Anne to put this chapter in the book, not to shock you, but to let you know that a person in a wheelchair has the same feelings, desires and needs as any other man or woman.

TELLING IT LIKE IT IS

Not long before I married Anne, a staff member mentioned my adopted daughter Susan. I was flabbergasted. Most of the staff thought Susan was adopted. When I talked to Anne, she admitted she had the same thought, that men in wheelchairs were impotent. At a staff meeting that morning, everyone learned that Susan was my biological daughter. I explained the difference between the sex life of a person with a spinal cord injury who has no feeling from the neck down, and one who lost his or her legs in war or lost use of them in an accident, through polio, or through another medical problem, but still has feeling throughout his or her entire body. I couldn't believe that Anne and most staff members were unaware of this. If all these people who had worked with paraplegics weren't aware of this fact, I reasoned that the general public was as uneducated on the subject. I explained that I had feeling in my entire body, but couldn't walk because polio had ruined the motor skills to my legs. Once Anne knew, she told me she loved me so much she had planned to marry me thinking I couldn't have sex, but was now looking forward to a great sex life when we were married.

SEX IN MARRIAGE IS A GIFT

After I had educated all of Goodwill's staff, Anne and I started discussing our coming marriage. I explained that I was concerned about what good Christian sex allowed. Since I had never heard any Christian men discuss sex in marriage, I reasoned that if Anne and the staff didn't think men in wheelchairs could have sex, most members of the church were probably of the same opinion. Anne didn't foresee any problems, but suggested I talk to Albert Fesmire, my pastor friend. It took a lot of courage on my part to make that call. Albert was delighted to have the opportunity to enlighten me that, at marriage, God blesses a good sex life and orders us not to withhold sex from each other. It was evident to Albert when he saw us together that Anne and I had a great love. He could see we were good friends who respected each other. In his opinion, maintaining our friendship was as important as maintaining our love. He told me to never let her doubt how much I love her, and predicted we'd have the best marriage of anyone he knew. His advice was for me to talk to Anne about sex now. If she felt it was "something she had to do" to be married, I should turn around and wheel in the opposite direction. In a good marriage, Albert felt the wife should be as enthusiastic about finding ways to strengthen and enjoy a good sex life as the husband. Each spouse has the responsibility to want to satisfy the other. He advised us to communicate, communicate, and communicate.

Before we were married, we had an appointment to talk to Denny Young, the pastor of our church to discuss our wedding and marriage. Because I had talked to Albert, I'm sure I surprised Anne when I asked Denny what he considered right or wrong for a married couple to do as far as sex was concerned. His advice was that anything the husband and wife agreed to do, with only each other, if it wasn't harmful or painful, has God's blessings. He reiterated Albert's advice on keeping romantic love alive during the days for happy nights. He also said, "Communicate, communicate, communicate!"

When Ken Shaw and I discussed what I should expect in a normal marriage, he too explained that women need to communicate for a good marriage. He felt that Anne and I wouldn't have any trouble having a great sex life since we truly loved and respected each other. He pointed out that we knew how to communicate.

When Anne and I started discussing married sex, she asked me to share my hang-ups with her, so I could work through them in a healthy way before we were married. I shared the following.

MY SEX LIFE BEGAN...

I remember when I first started feeling my manhood coming. I was young and still recovering from polio. One of my friends talked about something he had tried. He didn't know the name of it, but smiled as he described it, letting our friends and me know it was something that helped him relieve his tension. I suspect that each of us could hardly wait to get home and get into the bathroom to experiment. My experiment didn't relieve my tensions; it nearly got me killed. My dad opened the bathroom door at the moment I first started. Instead of talking to me about it, he made me feel like God was going to strike me dead. As if being seen by my dad wasn't bad enough, he told me he was going to have Mom talk to me. Of course, all of us thought that was a fate worse than God striking us dead. Since I wasn't thinking anything about sex with anyone,

I couldn't understand what the fuss was all about. It took me a long time not to feel ashamed of my masculinity. I don't remember accepting that as a blessing until after Anne and I were married.

MORE ABOUT MY SEX LIFE

When I was attending Wayne State University, I still remembered my bathroom experience. Dick Wooten, my roommate, told me I was normal, and to get over it. Whenever we were alone, Dick liked to embarrass me by talking about sex. Since I was so overly protected at home, it was probably good that I had the opportunity to hear some of the things he said. When he talked about what he fantasized his married life was going to be like, it sounded good to me, but my face turned crimson, or so he said. He was probably right.

After Anne agreed to marry me, I called Dick Wooten to tell him the good news. He reminded me how red my face was when he shared his sex fantasies with me at college. Dick advised me that I should not be ashamed of anything that Anne and I did after marriage, because God created us with the desire for each other. He emphasized that communication is as important in marriage as love, and suggested we tell each other what delights us. Both Anne and I believed in abstinence until marriage. I spent many months asking God to forgive me for being so normal, and wanting Annie so badly. I could hardly wait until we were married so I could experience a normal love life.

ANGELS AWARE

When I lived in an apartment before we were married, I was concerned about falling when I transferred to my shower chair. Usually when I showered, I would take the phone inside the bathroom and call Anne. She agreed to call 911 if I had any problems.

As our wedding drew near, unhappy memories in my past kept nagging at me. I was ashamed of how my body looked. I often saw Anne in a bathing suit near her pool; she had a gorgeous figure. Every time I looked into her starry eyes, I was sure our married life was going to be great.

Suddenly nagging doubts crept into my mind. What would happen if Anne decided she didn't want to be married to me, once she saw that my chest and back muscles were nearly flat? Because I had to wear the back brace to replace those muscles, my stomach had open scars where the back brace rubbed when I was seated. I felt my legs were too skinny. I couldn't stand it any longer. I felt I owed it to Anne to let her make that decision before we were married.

About two or three weeks before our wedding, I got up the courage, and asked Anne if she would come over to my apartment and sit in the dining or living room while I showered. I explained I would put on my briefs and wrap a towel around me after my shower.

Ever since I recovered from polio, I missed getting to lie on a blanket on the floor. I asked Anne if she would tip my wheelchair back so I could do that. I explained it would give her the opportunity to look at my chest, stomach, back and legs to see if she felt I was repulsive. Tears streamed down Anne's face when she told me she loved me, and asked me why I thought I had to prove anything to her. Her feelings were obviously hurt that I would even think she would feel that way.

Tears welled up in my eyes when I explained my fear. She hugged me and agreed to "come look my body over" if it would make me feel better. I promised that I'd wear my briefs and keep a towel wrapped around me. When I'm writing about it now, I'm convinced she must have thought I had lost my mind, but she was willing to humor me.

After my shower, I put on my briefs, but not my slacks, and wrapped a blanket towel around my waist and another around my shoulders and chest. I still had a blanket towel wrapped around my entire body as I leaned back. Anne gently put the back of my wheelchair down to the blanket on the floor. I pulled myself off onto the blanket. I pulled one towel up to uncover my legs. As I uncovered my chest, Anne's eyes twinkled, and I was thrilled by the pleased expression on her face. She touched my skin ever so gently and had me turn over onto my chest. She rubbed my back, purring as she told me how great I looked. She kissed the back of my neck, and said she loved how my hairy legs looked. She told me they were not too skinny; they were perfect. I felt so relieved at her acceptance of my body that I nearly cried for joy.

Before she could say anything more, a car pulled up, and someone knocked on my door. Anne said something about God sending His angel to keep us from temptation and quoted I Corinthians 10:13. Anne was laughing and couldn't understand why I felt shy. She pointed out that I not only had on briefs, but I still had the towel wrapped around my waist almost to my knees. She said I was more fully clothed than any man on a beach. Since Anne was fully clothed, she couldn't understand any reason to be concerned. She yelled that she'd be right there.

She helped me turn over onto my back and to sit up on the blanket. It was rather chaotic. Anne had moved my legs onto the chair, but was having trouble helping me to get my body lifted back into the wheelchair. I didn't have the strength to move over either. As Anne put the other blanket towel around my shoulders, and started to open the door, I felt vulnerable and horrified at the thought of anyone else seeing me clothed only in briefs and towels. I didn't want someone to get the wrong idea and hurt our reputations. We kept shouting for them to wait a minute. By the time we got me onto my chair and I rolled into my bedroom, the knocking stopped, and the car drove away. Like Anne said, anyone on the other side of the door, listening to us, probably had much worse thoughts of what was happening than they would have had if we had invited them in.

As I dressed in my room, Anne shouted how wonderful my body was, walked out of the door, and told me she'd call me when she got home. We decided Anne had been wise in not being alone in my apartment with me. I still have no idea who might have been knocking. Anne is convinced it was an angel. After that night, I could hardly wait for our wedding. Anne loved teasing me on the phone, warning me she wasn't sure I could control her after the gold was on our fingers, and she was Mrs. David Davey. I told Anne that I'd dreamt about that all my adult life, but had never experienced it.

The next day, I discussed that evening with Albert. When I asked him if he felt that I had been un-Christian in asking Anne to come over, he made me feel better. He told me I should not feel like I had done anything horrible because God knew my motive. He said I had shown real love because I cared about Anne's feelings, and that she had shown real love by trusting my motive in having her come.

MY "TOTAL MAN" EXPERIENCE

I was so disappointed that we were only home from our honeymoon for a few days when I had to go to a seminar for four days. By that time, I loved our new lifestyle. After our exciting honeymoon, I felt like I thought a "normal" man must feel, but Anne sensed I felt that something was missing. Before I left for the seminar, I told Anne about calling Dick Wooten before our wedding. I shared how Dick teased me about my red face in college when he shared his fantasies with me. When Anne asked what his fantasies were, I couldn't remember. She asked me what fantasies I had about our life. She wondered if there was anything I had always hoped to do, but thought would be impossible. We talked about it for an entire evening. By the time I told her everything I thought would be exciting, I think my brain and other parts were about to explode. We had fun that evening.

The next day, before I went up north to the seminar, I talked to Albert Fesmire and Ken Shaw. It was the first time I felt comfortable talking to them about sex. They both encouraged me to enjoy married life and to feel grateful for Anne's and my strong love. They also reminded me that all the desires that Anne and

I had for each other were those that God had created within us. I was surprised when they assured me that none of my fantasies were perverted because they had experienced them all. Finally, I felt good about myself.

What an exhilarating surprise when Anne called me at noon on Thursday, the last night I would be gone. She planned to leave work at 4:30 p.m., grab a hamburger, and join me after the two-hour drive. I loved her sexy voice as she told me to prepare for a "night of fantasies". Remembering the night before I came to the seminar, allowed my imagination to go crazy during the afternoon meetings. I'm sure I must have looked like a Cheshire cat. After the meetings, I had to go quite a distance outside the building to get to my room. I left the dinner meeting before it was over so I could soak my legs in the bathtub before Anne arrived. It was really cold up there in November. With poor circulation in my legs and feet, they were like ice. I was afraid they would freeze Anne. It was early, but dark, when she knocked on the door, saying, "Tiger, let me in. Grr-rrr." My heart pounded so loudly I was sure she could hear it through the door. I didn't really have to worry about my cold legs. It was only a short time before my circulation had me warm all over.

After we had fulfilled every fantasy I ever had, Anne told me of a fantasy I might want to consider, but she warned me that our shoulders and my knees, feet and muscles would probably hurt for a week. She told me to take time to think about it. What was there to think about? Pain seemed insignificant at the thought. Even in my wildest dreams, I had never given that possibility a thought. Afterward, I was convinced I had died and was already in heaven. For the two hours before my wake-up call, we slept a sleep of the totally satisfied.

As we were getting dressed, I knew I couldn't concentrate at the seminar, and was convinced that my smile was past ear-to-ear. I wanted to follow Anne to Goodwill to make sure we both got there safely. Anne's warning about pain the night before proved to be accurate, but in my pain I finally felt like a "total man." I sang all the way back to Kalamazoo.

When I returned to Goodwill, I was humming as I transferred out of the car, onto my wheelchair. My smile must have been obvious. When I wheeled into Ken Shaw's office, he smiled and let me know he wasn't even going to ask me what I had done.

A few weeks later I received a call from Albert. When I told him about my "total man" experience, he laughed heartily and told me to praise the Lord because his prediction was right. He said it was obvious that God was truly blessing this marriage.

THE MYTH LIVED ON

Four years after our wedding, I taught an adult Sunday School class at our church. Susan worked in the nursery. Someone made a comment about Susan being adopted. I once again explained the differences between my body and that of a person with a spinal cord injury. I shocked many of the class members when I shared some details about Anne's and my wonderful sex life. Most of the class members expressed their happiness at our good fortune and admitted they thought Susan was adopted. The next week, several of the members thanked me and told me they had an entirely different understanding of wheelchair users after my explanation. Later a class member called me for advice on his sex hang-ups.

RETIREMENT

After my retirement party in 2000, Anne told me she was sorry if she embarrassed me by what she said on the video that was played at the party. My question was, how any husband could mind if his wife loved him enough to say, "When I see a magazine that says, 'World's 10 Sexiest Men', I always ask, 'Where's Dave's picture?'" I assured her that I wasn't embarrassed, but I was so proud. How many women have the courage to let the world know they find their husband sexy?

After the event, when Anne stood talking to some women, one of them said something to her about her joking on the film. Anne assured the woman that she wasn't joking. A mutual friend spoke up and said, "Anne wasn't joking. That's how I feel about my husband Tom." The other woman was speechless. Anne and I have always been pleased that they also have that special relationship.

NEAR THE END: (WRITTEN BY ANNE)

Our master bathroom has a large roll-in shower with shower heads on both ends. On July 5, 2005, two days before Dave died, we thought he had fully recovered from the pneumonia that befell him on July 1st. Dave and I had such fun when we had a water fight while showering together. The large windows in the bathroom were open. Our laughter was so loud our neighbors must have wondered what was happening. It was a fun day. When Dave awoke on July 6th, feeling bad again, I asked him if he felt that he was worse because of the previous night. If so, did he feel we should consider giving up sex? He looked at me, and as weak as he must have felt, he smiled that wonderful smile of his. His eyes twinkled as he said, "Annie, if I ever answer, 'yes' to that question, call the coroner, because you'll know I'm already dead."

A FEW WORDS FROM ANNE

It is my desire that people who read this book will share the message of hope to anyone who has a crippling disease, comes home from the armed forces with an injury, or suffers from an accident of any type. Let them know that God created them, and they should not be ashamed of their body regardless of any disfigurement. God loves them the way they are.

If your spouse, family or friends love you, they don't define you by your body. Does the loss of legs or arms define your relationship with God, your integrity, your concern for others, your desire to belong to someone, your ability to love your spouse, your children, or your family?

No person, famous, rich or influential, has been more loved than Dave was by our children, grandchildren, relatives, friends, co-workers, total strangers that he made a difference in their lives, and me. He made a difference in our lives. Please spread the word that it is God Who gave you the desires of your heart whether you can run, walk, or need to use a wheelchair or motorized scooter of some type. May God bless you!

Chapter 23

Retirement

W<small>HEN</small> D<small>AVE</small> <small>AND</small> I returned from our memorable three-month trip to Alaska, I volunteered at Goodwill to assist Dave. His assistant retired during our trip. When the board of directors discovered I was volunteering, they temporarily hired me to help Dave. I also assisted them in planning Dave's retirement party.

In 1999, several months before Dave retired, the *Kalamazoo Gazette* wrote nearly a full-page article about his upcoming retirement. For the next eight months, many people who had been helped by Goodwill's programs visited him in his office, at our home, sent him notes or called him.

A MEMORABLE EVENT

Words alone cannot describe Dave's retirement party. The board of directors outdid themselves. Dave really appreciated all the work they put into making this event the success it was. It was held at Western Michigan University's Fetzer Center.

Robert Jones, Mayor of Kalamazoo, greets guests Mel and Gloria Visser at the door of Dave Davey's retirement dinner, with Gloria Romence, Community Leader, watching in background

Robert Jones, Mayor of Kalamazoo, was the greeter. Larry Braithwaite, owner of The Frame Maker, took hundreds of our photos and Dave's awards, and made a display that covered the two long walls of the reception area. It consisted of a ten-foot long and a fifteen-foot long three-dimensional photo collage. He used blue mounting board backing, raised to different depths, to set apart the photos and awards. These were mounted on five feet Styrofoam boards. One wall had ten feet of the display and held pictures and awards involving Goodwill and the community. His obelisk award, for winning the first Goodwill Industries International Distinguished Career Award, and ten or twelve of his award plaques were also on that wall in a separate 3-dimensional display. The other fifteen-feet striking display featured pictures of our family. What an awesome gift.

Two bagpipers play a march for David and Anne Davey to lead guests into retirement dinner at Western Michigan University

Two bagpipers provided music in the reception area for the hour that people were looking at all the displays. While playing a march, the bagpipers led all of us from the reception area into the party room. As guests found their seats, the bagpipers played "Amazing Grace," and marched out of the room as the last echoes of the song faded. This unique music was a gift from friend Jim Thorne.

Lori Moore and David Davey listen as Fred Grandy speaks

Lori Moore, our favorite Kalamazoo radio announcer at the time (now hosts a local TV variety show), served as the emcee of the event.

Fred Grandy, president of Goodwill Industries International at the time, but better known as Gopher on TV's "Loveboat," was the speaker.

Goodwill Board President Tom Schaberg, Radio/TV celeb and party Emcee Lori Moore, Speaker Goodwill International President Fred Grandy, David and Anne Davey at the head table for David's retirement party. Dave's family is seated in front on right

Tom Schaberg, Goodwill's board president and Dave's dear friend, presented him with a Service Award plaque from the Board of Directors. Dave also received several other awards.

Friend and State Legislator Dale Shugars presents a State Tribute to Dave Davey at his retirement party

A wonderful seventeen-minute video, a gift from Lawrence Productions, was shown. It included comments from past board members, our pastor, current and past staff members, local dignitaries, Congressman Fred Upton, and our family.

Back row—Anne Davey, Marilyn (Dave's sister) and Stan Zidel; front row—David Davey, daughter and son-in-law Susan and James Gibson

The entire evening was taped by our local TV Cable Channel, and played locally three times.

Fred Grandy with David and Anne Davey after Dave's retirement party

JULIE USES POETRY TO EXPRESS HER THOUGHTS

Our daughter Julie enjoys writing poems to express her feelings. The following poem was written to Dave when he retired.

The Retirement of David M. Davey

With no idea where this will lead
I ask you now, go on, and please read.
A rest from work has come to pass;
Vacations endless have come alas.
No eight to five traffic to fight.
Alarm clock's tossed. It's only right.

No more Goodwill for you to tend
The plaques and awards are soon to end.
A much-deserved rest is in store
Bound to keep busy, now probably more,
As all assume that retirement means
You've extra time, or so it seems.
Before you know it, you'll have a year
Behind you in the retirement sphere.
You'll look up again, glad to be alive
And realize that it has been five.
So take a week off anyway,
Or at least a weekend, or a day.

You've earned the time off. Read a book.

As flowers grow, take time to look.

Watch as tomatoes turn to red.

Get a piglet or two. Don't let it be said

You didn't try your hand at farming.

'Course neighbors may find this alarming

For now, at least take time to reflect

I'm sure all people will respect

A little time simply for leisure

To rest and relax just for pleasure.

So now, our wish is just for you

Happy retirement, and for now...Adieu!

Love always, Julie

RETIREMENT IS FINAL

On the last official day of Dave's employment, he and I were in Washington DC at the Goodwill Delegate Assembly. Dave received his forty-year pin, and introduced John Dillworth, his successor in Kalamazoo.

One of the highlights of the entertainment for the Delegate Assembly was an evening at one of the Washington DC art museums. The display included all originals from Norman Rockwell's museum. We saw every magazine cover he painted, and an original or copy of every other painting of his. It was a wonderful treat. To go to the display rooms, however, we and another CEO in a wheelchair had to take the freight elevator, located in the oldest part of the museum. It reminded Dave of the one that he rode in more than forty-five years before while he was attending classes at Cooley High School in Detroit.

EAST, NORTH EAST

When we left Washington, we spent the next two weeks traveling through the east coast of the USA and the southern part of Canada before returning home.

In Maine, we went whale watching one day. As the whale watching boat approached, we were shocked when we saw a young man who looked like he was in his twenties, sitting in a wheelchair, strapped to the outside front of the cabin of the boat. He looked like someone out of Homer's Odyssey. When the boat unloaded, before we were allowed to board, he was pushed off the boat by a friend. He was soaking wet, shivering, and looked very cold, but he yelled to friends on the dock, and told them it was an exhilarating experience, and he loved every minute of it. Even though it was July, it was cold out on the water. We felt badly for him, but when Dave talked to him, the man said it was the most thrilling experience of his life. He said he had always wanted to do it. He was unsuccessful when he encouraged Dave to try it. If the man didn't die of pneumonia, he had to be one of the healthiest men alive.

The cold air was chilling as we were waiting to board. Dave and I were inside the cabin during the entire trip and were still cold whenever anyone opened the door. How exciting it was to be sitting in the boat together, watching the many whales as they did their thing around our boat. It was such an experience when the guide would say, "Look any way you want. We have several whales at one, two, three, four, five, six, seven, eight, nine, ten, eleven, and 12 o'clock. What a sight."

LOVE BOAT

Dave's breathing was always improved when we were on water. He and I took a cruise on the Sun Princess in 2002. When we flew from the United States, we flew into Costa Rica. Because we were late arriving, we were quickly whisked off the plane to meet our van driver. Unfortunately, we left about twenty-thousand-dollars' worth of our camera equipment on the seat of the plane. We and four other late arrivals had to ride an hour to board the ship. When the van driver brought our luggage aboard, we noticed we had no cameras. The driver called the airport and told them to hold the equipment until the next day. The next morning the van was waiting at our next port. Not only was everything safe, but the case also held nearly one-thousand-dollars in cash. What a blessing. The man who found it on the plane was so thrilled with the reward. The van driver laughed and told Dave that was about twenty times the amount he was used to receiving. We were reminded that this was the cruise ship where Fred Grandy, the CEO of Goodwill Interna*tional, pla*yed Gopher on the TV show, "Love Boat". When we docked, Dave was unable to use the Princess tour busses. We hired private vans to drive us in Costa Rica, Panama, Columbia, and six other countries or islands. Three owners of the private vans took us to visit their homes. Each was proud of the fact that his house was totally wheelchair accessible.

Before we were married, I asked Dave if there were any trips he would love to take, but doubted that he ever could. He told me he had always dreamed about seeing Alaska, Hawaii, and the Panama Canal. This trip through the Panama Canal fulfilled the last of his dreams.

Neither Dave nor I was interested in shopping. Instead, Dave had the van drivers take us to the sites of their island where they took their house guests. We saw the most beautiful beaches, met wonderful natives, and learned the culture of each island. In Costa Rica we visited with the people who make the large, brightly colored wooden carts that are often in hotel lobbies. The factory is open to the air with only two walls, and still uses the small fast running creek for their power as they did over one hundred years ago. They still paint the lovely carts out in the open. Some of their carts are made for farmers to take their crops into the markets. We saw many carts along farm road that were drawn by oxen or other animals. Our guide took us to the open markets where residents eat. We saw a funeral procession walking down the road, with the casket being carried over the heads of twelve men. We attended the funeral service in a large Catholic church. Of course the service was in Spanish so we couldn't understand the message. As we sat there quietly, the funeral procession left the church for the burial. We were so surprised when we were approached by a local group of people who asked us if we would come to the front of the church and witness their daughter's wedding. The woman spoke very good English. Everyone we smiled at spoke to us in English.

When we arrived in Columbia, we were taken to Bogota to see a live play. It was well worth the trip. All the passengers who left the ship traveled in about thirty or forty buses and vans that stayed together as we rode into Bogota. As we exited the theatre, we were deluged with about one hundred people selling handsome leather belts for one dollar in American money, scarves, jewelry, and other beautiful items. Unfortunately, we had left almost all our money in the safe in our room. We were told to go directly to our bus or van and to go nowhere else. In Bogota, I was concerned when I noticed so many soldiers with bayonets on their rifles. When I asked a police officer about the reason, he let me know that we had never been safer than we were right then. He told us the city could not exist if it were not for the many tourists on the luxury liners. The soldiers were there for our protection. He also let us know that he didn't have enough soldiers to protect us if we drove ten miles in the other direction, from the city.

The citizens of Puerto Rico are so proud of their brick streets and sidewalks. However, they were difficult for wheelchair users to maneuver.

We ate at an Appleby's, and talked to many local residents having a good time. Unfortunately, we were unable to take a tour of the island because we had to catch our flight home.

"GOOD ENOUGH" IS NOT GOOD ENOUGH

It's good to see there are still advocates who share Dave's and his team's vision for needed changes. Although Dave and his staff had the opportunity to help many people find success, I can still hear Dave and Ken Shaw, nearly forty years ago, encouraging the staff, "Goodwill and other service providers must never be satisfied with the current program. They must continue to look for new programs and ways to help all the people who aren't employed." Dennis Frey also adopted this philosophy.

AND THE CHALLENGE CONTINUES...TODAY

Melanie Kurdys, a former member of the Portage School Board, reminded me a few years ago, that there is still much to do. She e-mailed me a note that read, "One of the on-going hurdles in implementing a barrier-free environment is 'old buildings'. Many schools have buildings, which are fifty years old or more, built when barrier-free was not yet part of building standards. A good example is the Portage Central High School. The connection between sections of one of the buildings has stairs access only. Wheelchairs are required to exit the building and use a sidewalk, in Michigan, where inclement weather is frequent. Of course, upgrading wheelchair accessibility is a high priority, but gaining voter approval for building funds is no small hurdle."

I'm pleased to report that a few years later, Portage voters approved a special millage to build several new schools, all of which are barrier-free.

Chapter 24

Awards

 IN HIS GOODWILL career, Dave received many awards, plaques, and wonderful letters. A few of those include:

LIFETIME ACHIEVEMENT AWARD

The Disability Resource Center of Southwestern Michigan presented the Jim Neubacher Lifetime Achievement Award to Dave at their annual meeting in 1999.

DISTINGUISHED CAREER AWARD

In 1991 Dave received a packet for the 1992 Conference of Executives. The literature informed him that a new annual award was going to be presented at the 1992 Conference of Executives in Albuquerque, New Mexico. It was the J.D. Robins Distinguished Career Award. Eligibility required having worked for Goodwill for twenty-five years, with a minimum of fifteen years as CEO.

Dave never told me the prize was a marble obelisk and one-thousand-dollars, when he threw the application into the wastebasket. He explained there was no need to send it in because there was an executive whose accomplishments were always in the national GOODWILL FORUM. He also told me of two other executives that deserved the award, but he figured the executive with the good communications department would certainly receive it. Dave said he could never expect to receive the award because there were so many other executives that had accomplished so much more than he ever had. Dave was a humble man who was always so busy working toward the next project that he never realized how much he did. Without Dave's knowledge, I filled out the form, and sent it in. Dave had been unable to attend the 1990 and 1991 conferences due to bad health resulting from his respiratory failure. He didn't plan to attend this one. He thought it was strange when he received two phone calls from Goodwill Industries International staff urging him to come and support the first recipient of the award. The local Goodwill was on a tight budget so Dave didn't feel it was appropriate to spend money for him to attend.

Only Fran Kirkpatrick, a past president of the Board of Directors of the local Goodwill, and a loyal friend of ours, knew I had submitted Dave's information. When I told her Dave had gotten a call from Goodwill in Washington, she insisted we go, and paid our expenses. Since she, her husband, their son, and their daughter had all served as Goodwill's Board President, she knew many of Dave's accomplishments. She felt confident that if I had submitted the application, Dave would win.

Pam Lynn, the wife of Albuquerque CEO Charles Lynn, hosted a very nice reception for the spouses of the CEO's attending the Conference. Bev Cooney, wife of the GIA office, urged all of us to attend the Awards Dinner since a new Distinguished Career Award would be given at the dinner to a deserving CEO. Many spouses weren't aware of it. I told them I was sure that all spouses of the fifteen eligible CEO's knew their husband was qualified. Although Dave didn't agree, I told them I felt Dave earned it, but that he had identified three others who especially deserved it. The wife of one of the three men named by Dave, spoke up and announced that she had a lovely niche built in their wall at home to display the obelisk. Many of the other wives spoke up and said their husbands had told them that the woman's husband would get the award. I said I was disappointed that GIA had already told her husband he was the winner. She denied that he had been informed, but smiled and asked if I ever read the GOODWILL FORUM. I agreed that her husband had accomplished a lot, but Dave knew of many outstanding projects done by other CEO's who, like Dave, didn't send in their accomplishments. I turned to the other two women and told them what Dave had told me about some great things their husbands had done. They nodded, but said their husbands never sent them in to the GOODWILL FORUM. The other wife came near me and whispered, "Anne, get a life." I laughed, and went over to ask Bev Cooney about her last vacation.

When I saw Dave later, he told me that one of the three CEOs he'd mentioned, had won because he announced at the meeting that his wife had a niche built in their home to hold the obelisk prize. I didn't mention that morning.

On the evening of the presentation of Awards, we sat at a corner table with other CEOs from Michigan and Michael Miller, the CEO of Portland, Oregon. These were all executives whom Dave highly respected. Harvey Kettering II, the chairman of the Nominating Committee, began by reading accomplishments that all of the executives had submitted. Later, when Mr. Kettering mentioned the national, state and local committees the winner had served on, Dave took notice. Others in the room were obviously disappointed.

He and I knew no other executive had served on all of them. When Harvey announced the winner was the only CEO to serve as chairman of the Conference of Executives for two years, Dave knew the award had to be his, but couldn't understand why he was even being considered. I leaned over and told him I had sent it in. His face became one big smile.

Only the executives from Michigan, at our table, knew of Dave's accomplishments; they smiled and nodded. Everyone else was looking around to see who had done all the things I had included. Harvey pushed Dave's wheelchair up the ramp to the table for Dave to receive his award. Never in Dave's wildest dreams did he think he'd ever receive the Distinguished Career Award. It totally overwhelmed him to find out that he was the first recipient of the award. He was quick to give credit for his accomplishments to Jesus Christ and to his excellent staff.

On the plane going home, Dave penned his version of I Corinthians 13, "Though I am honored by my colleagues in this life; and, though God has blessed me with a wonderful wife, three children, and two (*now five*) grandchildren that are perfect for me;

and, though God has blessed me with friends who love me in spite of my shortcomings; and, though God has blessed me with the best Goodwill staff and board members in the world; and, even if I can be a part of new programs that will affect lives in the future; and, though I share the media attention when my staff and board open Goodwill stores; and, though I am blessed when people approach me in grocery stores to tell me what Goodwill has done to change their lives; God, help me always to remember that if I do not have the love of Jesus Christ in all that I do, I am nothing. Now these three remain: Faith, Hope and Love, but the greatest of these is LOVE." Dave typed it and kept it in his wallet until he died. When I showed it to our daughter Susan, we could tell he had read it often.

GOODWILL INDUSTRIES HALL OF FAME

In February 2007, our granddaughter Lucy and I went to Las Vegas to accept the plaque for Dave's induction into the Goodwill Hall of Fame. The total number of members in the Hall of Fame at that time was forty men and women. Each was honored for their contribution to Goodwill in the century old agency. Michael Miller, the CEO of the Goodwill in Portland, Oregon, a man that Dave considered his friend and a man of integrity, nominated Dave. Our family really appreciates all the time and energy that Michael Miller and his assistant gave to make this possible. Dave's award reads"

"Dave Davey was a champion for people with disabilities. His personal experiences and observations led him to create innovative Goodwill programs such as a vocational evaluation system and sub-contracting opportunities for people with disabilities that saved partner employer organizations both space and money. As an advocate for the integration of people with disabilities in the workforce, Mr. Davey's work on the National Barrier-Free Architectural and Transportation Board helped develop the standards for the Americans with Disabilities Act in 1990.

Mr. Davey created many positive relationships with government disability agencies, and he was invited to be the first Goodwill Industries CEO on the Commission for the Accreditation of Rehabilitation Facilities (CARF). As the Executive Director or CEO in Goodwills in Sandusky, Ohio, and Battle Creek and Kalamazoo, Michigan from 1961–2000, he created the Michigan Association of Rehabilitation Facilities and was instrumental in creating regional and national venues for the sharing of best practices. He also shared rehabilitation knowledge and helped develop organizations around the world, notably the Goodwill affiliate in Zimbabwe."

LETTERS OF ENDORSEMENT

Michael Miller sent me the letters of endorsement that accompanied the nomination for Dave to be inducted into the Goodwill Hall of Fame. I contacted Leonard White and some of the Goodwill Industries (GWI) executives who wrote letters. Each has given me permission to include excerpts from her/his letter. These include:

> "Dave was a nurturing, supportive, mentoring supervisor. I had the opportunity to observe, first hand, a CEO that balanced requirements to meet the needs of people in the local community with the recognition that real influence, on solving local problems, included being pro-active and committed to participation with state and national influences. His vision was responsible for: revitalizing the Battle Creek Goodwill; building and developing programs at the Kalamazoo Goodwill; and was jointly responsible for development of national standards of accreditation (CARF). Dave not only encouraged his staff, but was a role model and mentor to others both in and out of Goodwills. His contributions included developing people, programs, agencies, organizations and standards."
>
> —Ken Shaw

"David was an outstanding executive who led a successful Goodwill Industries that was efficient, financially secure, and operating quality programs dedicated to the mission of helping people with disabilities and special needs. He was an innovative leader who led his life as well as his Goodwill Industries according to the highest standards of professionalism and integrity."

—Dennis Pastrana, President and CEO, Miami, FL

"David was always willing to provide information and advice and support. As I recall, David was a pioneer in the area of accreditation whether it was from GIA or CARF. David had a deep love for his job and for the clients and employees he served with disabilities. He was an inspiration to all and greatly loved by his board, community and staff."

—J. Larry Neff, President & CEO, South Bend, IN

"I had the opportunity to observe his leadership at national meetings, training events and on national committees. Attributes are many, his leadership and advocacy for persons with disabilities, his spirit and dedication, and his vision of how the movement could grow and expand services to persons with barriers to employment."

—Gayle Byrne, President/CEO, Medford, OR

"He was an outstanding role model. He may have had a physical disability, but his spirit and dedication to Goodwill was exemplary. I also appreciated his wonderful spirit of cooperation and congeniality. "Impossible" didn't seem to be in Dave's vocabulary or his life."

—Rex L. Davidson, President & CEO, GWI of Greater New York & Northern New Jersey, Astoria, NY

"As a person with disabilities, he understood first hand some of the very real physical and attitudinal barriers that many of our consumers work to overcome. He worked to break down those barriers in his community, in his state and at the national level. As Chair of the Conference of Executives, he modeled his servant leadership style long before it came into vogue. I never heard him say anything negative about a peer or staff member. He looked for the good in everyone, and everyone felt good in his presence. Sometimes it is easy to get caught up in the numbers and in "running the business." Through his life example, Dave reminded us that while content of accomplishment is important, content of character will have the longest lasting impact."

—Michael Elder, President & CEO, Charlotte, NC

"David had a passionate commitment to lead his Goodwill to new levels of success with a determined focus on the mission achievement. He has been recognized as an acknowledged leader through his service on the GII Board of Directors and Executive Council."

—Bruce Phipps, President and CEO, Roanoke, VA

"Dave was an advocate, a leader and a genuinely caring human being. As an advocate, he was a spokesman for people with disabilities through national, state, and local boards and advisory groups. Dave also played an important role in the development of the Americans with Disabilities Act. Dave served as Chair of the Conference of Executives for two terms, responding positively in a time when our organization needed him to lead. Dave was also a leader in the field of serving people with disabilities, and building programs that have been serving people with disabilities with quality services for many years."

—Michael S. Rowan, CEO, San Diego, CA

"I think Dave exemplified what I envision a "Hall of Famer" being—a long, rich, and productive history in the Goodwill movement, a genuine concern for people, and a

legacy—things he left and people whose lives he touched—
that made him the special person he was."

—Bob Holderbaum, CEO, Battle Creek, MI

"As an employee and officer of the W K Kellogg Foundation
from 1946 through 1980, I was in charge of the Foundation's
grants to agencies providing aid to the Handicapped. In
that capacity I ended up working closely with Dave Davey,
Executive Director of Goodwill Industries in Battle Creek
for several years. Dave assumed that assignment when the
Battle Creek Goodwill was at the worst possible low ebb,
and he performed miracles in its revival. Dave was a most
competent administrator and had a genuine interest in and
feeling for employees of his agency, in particular seeing them
being employed in the private sector.

"When Dave became CEO in Kalamazoo, I marveled at
Dave's expertise expanding to committees and Boards of
associations in Michigan, and then the United States."

—Leonard L. White, Vice President Emeritus,
W K Kellogg Foundation

I believe these endorsements all confirm that David Davey
fulfilled his purpose in life.

Ken Shaw also was inducted into the Goodwill Hall of Fame in
2007. Ken died a week later in Florida. His precious wife Connie
and I recognize our husbands did everything they could to make
America barrier free and to provide services necessary to make it
possible for people to be able to work.

Chapter 25

Hospitality

AVE AND I enjoyed entertaining guests in our home. We were youth leaders for three years when our children were teenagers, so we were truly blessed. We always had a houseful of young people daily. Our basement became everyone's recreation room. There were weights, two pool tables, a foosball table, a ping pong table, and tables for playing Monopoly, Scrabble, cards, or any game they chose to play. Occasionally the boys carried Dave downstairs for part of the evening. Otherwise, many of the youth would come upstairs to sit and talk to Dave. Usually, there would be one other mother and I serving refreshments downstairs or just being there for anyone who needed to talk. The youth group called it the poor man's country club.

Many Sundays, we invited church members to dinner. We were able to get to know the members this way.

We hosted missionaries, guest speakers and singers, and many others who needed a Christian place to sleep.

COLLEAGUES INTERNATIONAL

For years we worked with Colleagues International, (at the time, they were part of the Kalamazoo Chamber of Commerce), to host business men and women from other countries. Usually there was a group of six to twenty people arriving in Kalamazoo on the same plane. They were with host families for one to five weeks. Some were from Third-World countries. Hosts were introduced to them at an assigned location; sometimes at the airport, or sometimes at a Colleagues International meeting, before we drove our one or two guests to our home.

It was our responsibility to see that our guests: (1) had a bedroom; (2) ate three meals a day; and (3) were driven to and from local businesses where they learned how American businesses were run. Usually, the host business provided lunch for them.

Anne Davey, Asya Volokhina and editors from two of the largest Ukranian newspapers celebrating Asya's birthday in our home

UKRAINE

Colleagues' staff and volunteers usually hosted the entire group for two days in Chicago. Dave and I enjoyed doing something special for each guest if their schedule allowed. Two young men we hosted were from the Ukraine. One ran a radio and television station; the other was in management of a computer business. During an ice storm, I picked up Thad at a local radio station, returning home via Sprinkle Road. The car in front of us and I were traveling at 20 mph when the other car hit a sheet of ice, spun around, and ended in a ditch. We were quite a distance behind; I slowed down but when we came to the ice, we slid and hit the other car before coming to a stop. A policeman was beside us in less than a minute. He had called the Police station to have the street closed behind us. After a few minutes, he had a tow truck pulling the other car out of the ditch, and then came to my side of the car.

I introduced him to Thad. The policeman smiled, shook Thad's hand, and was very nice as he welcomed him to the United States, Michigan, and Kalamazoo County. He told us he had seen everything, and there was nothing either driver could have done to prevent the occurrence. There would be no tickets issued. He smiled again as he told Thad that he was glad we weren't hurt, and that it was only a "fender bender". He told us to follow him as he drove to the Portage city limits, where the roads were cleared and salted.

The next morning, Thad and I were doing a 30-minute live interview at a local radio station. Thad explained that he had been in a "fender-bender" the previous evening. He said he was sorry that my car was now in the garage, but he was pleased that he had met a local policeman, who was so courteous. He assured the interviewer that we would have sat there for hours if we were in the Ukraine. Thad loved the term "fender bender" and used it many times during his visit.

The other young man was able to spend three days with a friend who worked in New York City. When he returned home, he told his friends in the Ukraine all about the Twin Towers, from the lower basement to the roof. Ten months later on September 12th he called and told Dave he had heard about the planes crashing into the Towers on the 11th. Everyone he knew cried when they heard about the terrible tragedy of so many lives being lost.

After Dave told our guests that we wanted to do something special for them in two weeks when they had four free days. He offered the men the opportunity to spend three days either in Canada or Washington D.C. They chose Canada. Dave drove them to Detroit to get Visas to enter Canada. While they waited on the Visas to be processed, they walked for four hours to get the feel of the famous city of Detroit. They told Dave they had walked for miles. After they picked up their Visas, Dave drove them to other sites in Wayne County that they hoped to see.

Because Dave had to attend an unexpected business meeting and was unavailable, my friend Lisa Teeter, and I drove them to Niagara Falls and Toronto, Canada. We arrived on the Friday after Thanksgiving in time to see the Christmas light display illuminated. The men had never seen so many lights and were amazed that the Falls could provide that much energy. In their cities, they often have power outages. We ate, then left them at the Falls to do their walking.

When Lisa and I returned to our hotel, Lisa was showering while I fell asleep immediately. A few hours later, Lisa shook me awake and, in a desperate whisper, told me to lie on the floor, by my bed. As soon as I did, I heard the commotion outside our room that had awakened Lisa. One man was threatening to go into his room to get his gun and shoot someone. It sounded like several guests were arguing about someone who had been winning at the casino. Obviously one of his friends had given him some bad advice, and he experienced a bad loss. He was mad, beyond words.

Lisa called the concierge. He told her not to call the police, and we soon heard him as he calmly talked to the loud group. He offered to let the local police settle the disagreement. The tone of the discussion calmed down, and following silence, the group thanked the concierge and went to bed. At breakfast, our guests told us that they walked until every store in the city was closed. They thought it was around 4:00 a.m. when they returned to their room. As soon as they finished eating, they were asleep in the car, on the way to Toronto.

In Toronto, they left to walk when we dropped them off early in the morning and, at 5:00 pm, they met us at the CN Tower for our dinner reservations.

They were amazed at the bargains they had been able to buy with the American money they had exchanged from Ukraine money when they arrived in the USA. Lisa and I felt that the items we bought were more reasonably priced in Canada than in the United States, and at the time, I believe the exchange rate was $1.35.

David and Anne Davey eating Christmas dinner at Grace Miller home

LUXEMBOURG

Another guest that came to visit, Claude Wiseler, the Mayor of the City of Luxembourg and Treasurer of the country of Luxembourg, was a guest for over a week. Luxembourg had a two-year college, and was in the process of building a four-year university.

*Anne is listening while Claude Wiseler explains
that Luxembourg is a Grand Duchy.*

Because Claude was a politician, Dave felt we should have one of our political friends over for dinner to talk with him. Dave had great respect for Dale Shugars, a State legislator at the time.

As soon as the two men were introduced, we learned that Claude was not here to learn anything about building universities, but about the Student Exchange program. Luxembourg was considering American universities sending their students who were seeking a degree in Finance to Luxembourg in exchange for the university basketball students from Luxembourg to come here to play. Dale was enthusiastic about taking Claude to meet the sports directors of universities in Michigan and Indiana. Dave couldn't have planned a better match.

RUSSIA

One woman from Russia was here for two weeks. On a Saturday when the visitors weren't scheduled for anything official, our church had a Teachers' Training seminar. Two hours of the program was a video for teaching by singing with children. Our guest noticed that all the material noted that it was leadership training material, thus allowing her to use it as official training material for the fourteen leaders under her supervision. Once the leaders attending the seminar at our church were aware of her need for fifteen packets, Dave and I joined about twenty attendees who were willing to give her their leadership packet.

About four months later, we received an e-mail from Europe, telling us that the Russian leaders loved the videos and learning the American language with children's songs like "The B-I-B-L-E" and "Jesus Loves Me."

HIGH-FLYING BALLOON

On November 12th, the first day of deer season, my friend Nancy Helmic, of another host family, and I took the two women we were hosting up for a Hot Air Balloon ride. Since we chartered the balloon, we were able to leave at around six a.m. The sunrise was breathtaking. As we were searching for live animals, two deer shot out from under some trees. Our people were taking pictures and yelling at the deer when an irate hunter came out of a deer blind with a long gun. He was yelling and cursing us for scaring away the deer; he had been in the blind for hours in order to get the perfect shot. We quickly left the scene.

We found ourselves quite high in the sky, making it possible for us to see a large organic Goat Farm in the distance. A woman was sitting on a stool outside, milking the goats. One of our guests yelled, "Are those real red apples on the tree tops in November?" Sure enough, they were. Our pilot lowered the basket where we could be heard. We yelled and asked the woman if she minded our picking the apples if we did not damage the trees. She quickly told us to help ourselves. We leaned over and picked many of the large red beauties.

From there, we went over the Allegan Forest. At a later site, we spotted a large pond with floating lily pads in full bloom of beautiful white blossoms. Who could believe that water lilies could be blooming in Michigan on November 12th? The guests leaned over and scooped up one or two.

Finally, the balloon pilot headed back toward Kalamazoo. He found a farmer's large barnyard and landed the balloon. We quickly jumped out of the box and helped to stop the balloon. The balloon was folded and put in our follow-truck, while an employee quickly spread tablecloths and set out treats for all. The company also provided each of the women with a bottle of Michigan non-alcoholic grape juice to take back to Ukraine with them. The apples were also taken to Ukraine by our guests. Somehow the women were blessed by U.S. and Ukraine Customs allowing them to bring the fruit home. I'm of the opinion that the U.S. Customs allow no fruit or plant to enter the country through Customs. The fear of something contaminating American fruit or vegetables would be very bad for our country.

Dave and Anne Davey join guests
and host families at Kalamazoo Airport

KALAMAZOO GOSPEL MISSION

Before we retired from our jobs, we wondered what we would be doing for the rest of our lives. Dave and I often talked of the different areas where we thought God might be able to use us. We hadn't officially retired when offers started coming. Immediately Dave was offered opportunities to serve on many boards, locally and nationwide. I was already performing "The Witness of the Innkeeper" in churches, senior centers, nursing homes, Christian schools, on ships, and more. Before I officially left Goodwill for the final time, our friend, Gloria Romence, introduced us to the Kalamazoo Gospel Mission Auxiliary members.

Janie Reed was a fun guest at our party. She has been a close friend since we were in the Gospel Mission Auxiliary.

I attended monthly meetings and was soon an officer. Dave made many phone calls, and sent notes to remind people of our meetings and the special events that the Auxiliary hosted for the people living at the Mission. He and I bought thousands of gifts over the years for men, women, and children for Valentine's Day parties for the mothers and children, as well as the Christmas parties for the men. We co-hosted a large auction for the Kalamazoo Gospel Mission, and did very well. God continued to use us to serve His people.

DINNER PARTIES

Both Dave and I had the same dream one night. God told us both to start having monthly dinner parties where we would invite fourteen adult guests, mostly from church. We had never considered our dining and living rooms big enough to hold fourteen guests. However, God told us how to set up the tables, what games we would play, prizes, and the food to serve.

Barbara Langston and Adrienne Fisher listen to Louise Rice's report

It didn't seem crowded and we believe everyone had a good time. No attendee ever refused a second or third invitation. Although the party was supposed to be from six to nine p.m., many people stayed until midnight.

Janette Warren talks to her partner as Adrienne Fisher and Louise Rice talk with Jo Lynn Palmer

MIKE AND ADRIENNE FISHER

Mike and Adrienne Fisher came to a party on the Friday after they first attended Oakland Drive Christian Church. Adrienne had a newly broken leg from an on-the-job car accident. She worked for the Secretary of State's office, and tested a person who had lost his driver's license, and wanted to restore it. Adrienne's leg was broken when the man lost control of his car and hit a tree. Adrienne needed to have her leg propped up, so she sat on the couch. We never heard if the man's license was restored. The broken leg didn't stop her enthusiasm. Mike and Adrienne were loved by everyone attending.

Mike and Adrienne Fisher watch Louise Rice and Ray Warren discuss the Gull Lake Bible Conference, where Ray was the Director.

Dave asked them to consider being our co-host and hostess. They agreed and did a super job for many parties. We began by inviting only people from church. After a year or so, we sometimes included personal and business friends as well.

Our friends Mike Fisher, Andy Hoekstra, Mary Mulder, Asya Volokhina, Kathy Vander Ploeg Hoekstra, County Commissioner Nasim and Rashida Ansari at our Valentine Party.

Adrienne joined the Worship Team at church immediately and often sang a solo special. Mike soon expanded his service to include giving the messages at a senior living facility on Sunday afternoons while Adrienne led the music, often singing a special. Dave and I tried to attend all of their services, which were powerful.

THE LANGSTON FAMILY

When Dave and I returned from Alaska, I worked for him at Goodwill since he only had one year before retirement, and his office staff had taken other jobs during his absence. We were told that Cornelius and Barbara Langston's young son had drowned in a local lake while we were gone. I had never met them before, but Barb soon became close friends to Dave and me. Barb seemed like my daughter. She had the children call us Grandma and Grandpa. We were so blessed.

Barb and Cornelius worked in the Contract department at Goodwill, doing very important contracts. Barbara made motors for Stryker Surgical Instruments. Barbara had been "Worker of the Year" for her extraordinary work record.

*Mike Fisher, Tim and Brenda Bowers, Cornelius and **Barb Langston**, Adrienne Fisher and friends at Barb's birthday party*

In the summers after we retired, we often took care of their three youngest children while Barb was at work. We took them to: pizza parlors, volunteer at the Kalamazoo Gospel Mission, movies, the Air Zoo, Battle Creek Zoo, the Portage City swimming lake, and so many other activities.

The children had never had a real vacation, so I invited Barbara and the children to be my guests at Niagara Falls, Canada, one of Dave's and my favorite cities. It was before Americans had to have a passport to travel in Canada. The men stayed home and worked. I rented an apartment with a sauna. We went on the "Maid of the Mist," the boat that goes near Niagara Falls; flew over the Falls in a helicopter; walked behind the Falls; bought season tickets to a large water park similar to Sea World, where we daily rode the many rides and attended sea animal shows; and the boys spent hours driving mini racecars around the world's largest race track for those cars. We gave each person the opportunity to select their favorite restaurant for one evening meal. Every morning each person was given a new disposable camera with 36 exposures to take pictures of anything they chose. Everyone had a great time, carefully choosing each subject.

The night before we left Niagara to return home, Barb was packing the trunk when she yelled for me to come around to the other side of the car quickly. She pointed to a huge wolf that was coming through the woods next to our apartment. I ran inside to make sure the children did not come out, and Barb jumped into the car and honked. As soon as the wolf turned around, Barb came inside and we decided to pack in the morning.

On the way home, Barbara and I asked the children what they enjoyed the most. Barb thought they would say "the waterpark or the helicopter ride." I thought they would say "riding the Maid of the Mist or the racecars." We were both surprised when the three children said, in unison, "We liked the sauna!"

The following week I had the film developed and four copies of each picture made to put into memory scrapbooks I made for each of them to remember their first trip.

They often came for holidays.

Front row—Barbara and Chevelle; Middle row—Cornelius, Manny and Kashira Langston Back row—Santa and Dave Davey Christmas 2000

I still cherish the cards that Barb gave us. They were all cards meant for a mother and father. From the day we met her, Dave and I felt like she was our daughter.

Ivory, her caregiver, called to say that he had called an ambulance because Barb was worse than she was the day before when I last saw her. I was numb as I *was* praying for my dear daughter, "God protect Barb and bless her with peace as she comes home to You." It's been over two years ago when God took her home, out of pain. I did the eulogy at her Celebration of Life. I miss you Barb. So do your kids. Tell Dave I send my love.

THE BEST YEARS OF OUR LIVES

Dave was on several national committees with the Oscar winning actor, Harold Russell. They soon became life-time friends. Many organizations had them both as guest speakers at the same conferences.

On December 8, 1941, the day after the attack on Pearl Harbor, Harold joined the U.S. Army as an instructor in the Parachute

Corps. He was working as an explosives expert in 1944 when a defective fuse exploded a charge of TNT he was holding as he instructed a demolition squad at Camp Mackall, N.C. Both of his hands were amputated.

Harold, whose hands were replaced with hooks, was featured in an Army documentary, "Diary of a Sergeant" which shared the rehabilitation of an amputee. Director William Wyler and Producer Sam Goldwyn saw the documentary, and offered the role of Homer Parrish in "The Best Years of Our Lives" to Harold.

The 1946 film depicted how WWII veterans coped with the aftermath of the war and their return to changed families and community.

With the world finally out of war, Americans loved the film. It won seven Academy Awards. Harold received two Oscars for the film: one as Best Supporting Actor; and a second, special Oscar for "bringing aid and comfort to disabled veterans through the medium of motion pictures." Although Harold had other roles in films and TV, his heart wasn't in acting.

Instead, Harold soon joined Dave and Harold Wilke (the man born with no arms), as they chose to be pioneers, spending most of their lives as advocates for the rights of the disabled. President John F. Kennedy appointed Harold as vice chairman of the President's Committee on Employment of the Handicapped. In 1964 President Lyndon Johnson made him Chairman, and Richard Nixon reappointed him as well. This opened many doors for Dave and everyone who was working for rights of the disabled. Dave got together with Harold every chance he could.

When Harold told Dave that he and his wife were going to be in Kalamazoo on a Thursday afternoon and evening, Dave asked him if they were free to come for lunch at our home, and offered to pick them up at the airport or hotel. Harold said he was delighted to finally come to our home. It turned out to be the Thursday before we had a monthly party planned for Friday evening. On the morning they were coming, Dave cooked four racks of baby-back ribs like those we served at our parties. He planned to have any leftovers available for guests to take home the following evening. Dave kept the ribs in the warmer while he drove his van to pick up Harold and Betty. I was busy making a huge salad and frying six skinless chicken breasts to slice and place on the salads.

When the van arrived, Dave parked in our wide driveway. Harold opened the door for Betty. I had just opened the screen door and waved at them when our neighbor, Helen Hnilo, who lived across the street screamed, "Oh my gosh! That looks like Harold Russell!" A friend of hers yelled, "Hi Homer Parrish." I wondered who Homer Parrish was.

Before Harold could answer the women, a man leaning out of the window of his red truck shouted, "It **is** Harold Russell." The man's truck was parked on the street in front of the house next door, and he was visiting with our neighbors, Don and Dee Campbell. Dave came down on his chair lift and shouted to everyone, "Come on over so I can introduce you." By that time, Harold, his wife Betty, and Dave were out of the van, and Dave had closed the doors with his remote. When the older man got out of his red truck, it was obvious that he had a problem with his leg. He hobbled over, following Don and Dee; Helen and her friend crossed the street as I came outside; and the driveway seemed to be full of people. Dave invited everyone to come inside the house where there was air conditioning. After everyone was introduced, the man visiting next door was pleased to share the fact that early in 1944, he was a paratrooper on a certain base, and had taken a class from Harold. Both men remembered a lot of facts about that class and base. They reminisced about some of the military staff that they both remembered. The man said he had survived combat in WWII, but had lost a leg when the military Jeep he was riding in turned over, a few weeks after the war had ended.

Everyone was talking at once about the great job Harold did as Homer Parrish. Dave and I had never seen the movie, "The Best Years of Our Lives." It was evident that everyone else had.

Dave looked around and told our guests that we would be having a dinner party the following evening, and suggested that it would be fun if we proceeded to have our own luncheon party right now. Everyone gladly agreed to stay.

Since Dee and Don had been to one of our parties, Dee picked up the glass jar full of candy to explain that each person guesses how many pieces of candy are inside, and the one guessing the closest, over or under, takes the candy jar home. Everyone seemed to be paying close attention to her explanation.

The salad plates were on the table when Dave asked a blessing for the food. If I remember correctly, one or two guests claimed to be vegetarians, but everyone ate the slices of chicken breast on their salad. While the salad was eaten, Dave served the hot ribs, with rice and asparagus, onto dinner plates. Dee removed the empty salad plates as I was serving the main course. Don placed a large platter of the remaining ribs in the center of the table. The platter was emptied and removed before Betty Russell helped Dee to serve the homemade cherry pie and ice cream. I filled the dishwasher, and dinner was over.

Everyone left the dining room and chose a chair in the living room to proceed with the party. Dave took a stack of the small papers and gave one to each guest and said, "Let's play game number one—the Candy Jar. Dee did a good job explaining this first game. Thanks Dee." On the small papers, there was a line for a name and one for the number of pieces of candy. The jar contained nearly four hundred pieces. The man who owned the red truck guessed the closest, and was thrilled when Dave handed the full candy jar to him. He was the only one that noticed the clear sealed glass top was full of red hots. Everyone else had guessed under 200.

The man held the jar of candy close to his chest. Tears were pouring down his face when he told us that he had never before won anything in his life. He also told us how very thrilled he was to be able to have had a delicious dinner, sitting next to a star like Harold Russell. A few of us teared up after Harold stood up and, with his hooks, gave the man a big hug.

The second game was a different form of White Elephant. Instead of our guests bringing a fun gift, we furnished them. Dave had wrapped many gifts purchased for weddings, showers, birthdays, gag gifts, etc., but, for some reason, they were never given. I was surprised when many expensive gifts were opened and appreciated, but the prized gift seemed to be a special fishing lure that two of the men had been wanting for over a year. I don't remember who got to take it home.

When the last game was played, Betty Russell reminded Dave that it was time for him to take them back to their hotel so they could prepare for their evening meeting. We had laughed, cried, and shared many facts of our lives during this party. With a former war colleague reminding Harold of past experiences, Harold even surprised his wife with some of the discussion.

We all walked Harold and Betty to the van, and hugs were enjoyed by all. Harold sounded very sincere when he spoke up and stated, "Dave, this is the very best dinner party we have ever attended." Betty said, "I was thinking the same thing." Everyone else agreed. When Dave returned, we spent the evening cleaning up and preparing for the party the next day. Until the day Don Campbell died, Don, Dave, Dee, and I often talked about that "extra fun dinner party."

Harold and Betty Russell with Dave and Anne Davey at the 1994 Kalamazoo Mad Hatters Annual Community Breakfast

When Harold Russell was the speaker at The Mad Hatters Annual Community Breakfast in 1994, he requested that Dave and I would be his invited guests. He told several guests about the early dinner party. Although I never saw Harold or Betty after that breakfast, Harold and Dave kept in touch with each other until Harold's health was bad. Harold and Betty died in 2002, Harold was eighty-eight. Dave considered Harold one of his favorite unsung American heroes for his lifetime spent helping handicapped persons to be employed.

Chapter 26

Lasting Memories

cA<small>FTER</small> D<small>AVE</small> <small>RETIRED</small> in 2000, he continued to team teach a Sunday school class of fifth and sixth graders at Oakland Drive Christian Church in Portage, Michigan. He served on distribution panels for the Greater Kalamazoo United Way, and felt blessed when he was asked to serve on the Executive Search Committee for the Disability Resource Center.

Granddaughters Jessica and Maegan Gibson,
celebrating Jessica's 5th birthday at our home

He made many phone calls for the Kalamazoo Gospel Mission Auxiliary. He continued to teach a Bible study in our home until the week before he died. Dave made many phone calls to friends he knew who were sick or dying. He searched the newspaper for articles about his acquaintances, and wrote them letters of congratulations or encouragement, whichever was appropriate. Up to the day of his death, many professional friends continued to call him and ask for his prayers or advice.

In the seven months before his death, Dave spent nearly twenty hours a day in bed, but was busy on his laptop computer and telephone. He never complained of pain, and was always his cheerful self. Once or twice a week I drove the van, and we went to dinner down in Amish country in Indiana, or we drove around this part of Michigan, looking at God's creation. We purchased extra respiratory equipment so we always had equipment in the van if it was needed.

Never has a wife been as blessed as I. David loved the Lord, his family, friends, and everyone that God put into his life.

Dave was sick with pneumonia on July first through July fourth, 2005. On the evening of the fourth, he had some visitors. On the fifth he felt great and really did too much. He worked in the computer room most of the day, trying to finish up the last verses of the book of Romans for our Bible study on the seventh.

On July sixth, Dave coughed up a lot of the pneumonia residue still in his lungs. It exhausted him so he put the head of his bed up quite a bit and rested most of the day. Finally, he felt better, was hungry, and ate a decent dinner. Near midnight Dave said he felt he had cleared his lungs and could talk, without coughing. He asked me if we could just sit up and praise God for all He had done for our family and us. He had the head of his bed up in a sitting position. I put the foot of my bed into a sitting position, and we sat facing each other and holding hands. What a delightful time we had for four hours and twenty minutes, praising God for our children Julie, Susan and David, our grandchildren Lucy, Philip, Maegan, Jessica and Joshua, our parents, family members, friends, church members, staff members, and individuals that Dave felt had helped change lives, locally, in-state and nationally. He named those who had personally made our lives better, including Tanya Downs, his barber who had faithfully driven fifteen miles to our home every month to cut his hair; Dennis Young, our pastor and friend; Dr. Thomas Abraham and his staff; Roger Joyner, our contractor and friend; Sam O'Brien, our garbage man extraordinaire; and the list went on.

Finally, at 4:20 a.m. on July seventh, Dave told me he was getting tired and would like to see if he could get some sleep. He wanted to be rested so he could get up for the Bible study that afternoon. We put our beds down, and I moved into his bed and rested my head on his shoulder, the way I did every night. We held hands. Three times Dave said in an almost urgent tone, "Oh Annie, I love you so much." Each time I responded with, "I love you David my darling." He kissed my forehead and I kissed his chin and neck. I heard him relaxing. Within minutes I could tell by his breathing he was sleeping comfortably, and I promptly fell asleep. When I awoke at 5:40 a.m., I found my precious David had gone home to be with our Lord. He looked so peaceful.

After I held Dave in my arms, crying and talking to him, I called Susan and Dennis Young, our pastor. Shortly after I called nine-one-one, the house was full of police, firemen, and friends of Susan and mine. I called Julie and David who lived on the West coast, and Lucy, our granddaughter who lived in Spain, overlooking the Mediterranean Sea.

Within a few hours, the radio and TV stations began announcing Dave's death and continued to announce it on News all day. The Kalamazoo Gazette newspaper called to get the information they needed to run articles that day and the following days. The phone rang all morning. Shirani Wijay, my doctor and friend, called to say her husband had heard about Dave's death on TV. She had me come right over to her office. She gave me a hug and told me that Dave and I were always holding hands and laughing together when she and her husband ate at the same restaurant as we. She said it was very important for my health that I continue to find things to laugh about. She knew Dave would want that. Sue and I were standing out in the front yard around 10:00 a.m. when the garbage truck pulled up. Sam O'Brien jumped out and came over to give us a hug. A customer on the lake near our home, came out and told him she had just heard on TV that David Davey had died.

That afternoon, I called our twelve-year-old granddaughter, Maegan. Maegan told me she hadn't cried yet. Then she said, quite seriously, "Grandpa talked to me recently and told me it might not be long before he would go to Heaven. I can't cry when I think about him being in Heaven running around. If he wasn't a Christian, then we'd really have something to cry about, wouldn't we Grandma?"

DAVE'S FINAL MESSAGE TO HIS FRIENDS

Dave had shown me on his computer where he had planned his Celebration Service if he died before I did. He wrote it on July 14, 2002, and revised it on February 1, 2005. He was cremated. We had his service ten days after his death. The church was crowded. Dave had hoped that we would have a joyous celebration where everyone left singing instead of crying. It was hard, but we followed his plan. He wrote a page, "When that time comes…" He instructed us to give it to those people who came to the service. He asked us to have them take it home and read it.

DAVID MEAD DAVEY
Born August 23, 1936
Died July 7, 2005, at home, at approximately 5 a.m.
Respiratory Failure

When that time comes ….

July 14, 2002
Rev. Feb. 1, 2005

A TIME OF JOY AND CELEBRATION.

"The one true God, our heavenly Father and Creator of the universe, sent His only begotten Son, Jesus, the Christ (Messiah), to die the sacrificial death, not to cover over our sins, but to totally obliterate sin, including our sins. Further, in the Scriptures, He promises to do the same for everyone who decides to accept this free gift and believe that He, Jesus, alone has the power and right to do so.

"While still a boy He cleansed me, securing me as a child of God, making me a part of His Bride, the Church, changing me as I went through my life on this earth. It was not I living the "Christian life", but Jesus living His life through me. "I" have not always lived out God's best plan for my life, but in His love and as He promised, He has forgiven me. Thank you, Jesus.

"Oh how my heart aches, however, over those times I failed you, Jesus, when in the presence of the people I desired to have place their trust in you and turn over their lives to you, I did not tell them of Your great love for them. God forgive me. Send someone else to show them Your love and forgive fullness."

"My somewhat questionable body has ceased to operate here on earth, and I am, forever, standing in the presence of my Savior, Jesus. I was told that many doctors told my parents I probably would not survive my twenties, if that long. Since 1948, when I was age twelve, was an epidemic year for my type of Polio, death claimed most in less than a decade. But God had His plan and His timing.

"I finished high school in a wheelchair, along with the young people with whom I attended grade school. Also, though it had never been done before, the high school principal, who lived on our street, asked for and received permission for me to attend Cooley H.S. the last two years. Mom was very persuasive. I was president of my graduating class of 600 students, and graduated from Wayne State University. I was blessed to work forty years with Goodwill Industries, retiring in 2000.

"In 1989 I suffered respiratory failure, was in the hospital two months and gradually returned to work over the following four months. God wasn't done with me even then. So you see why I can say, "This is a time not only for joy, but <u>great</u> joy."

"It would be my delight that some people who have known me on earth might gather for a time, not in sadness, but in celebration, to praise Jesus and sing of His love and promises that were the major force in my life. I hope Dennis Young, God's special servant, is available to preach "Jesus" as he has so faithfully through his ministry and personal testimony.

"I grew up in a family that believed in and talked openly about Jesus Christ. One of the greatest impacts on my life was remembering my mom praying for me and my brother and sisters. I knew she kneeled by her bed, calling out to God on our behalf. I could not hear her words but knew she was pleading with God to make Himself so real in our lives that we could not refuse to give our lives to Him.

"Most familiar is the hymnology of the 1940's–60's, while not forgotten, is sung less often than the songs of today. Probably most dear to me is "Amazing Grace", all four stanzas, a favorite of my maternal Grandfather (known as Bumpa) and of my Mom, Helen, whom some may have met. She was the pipe organist at age twelve, and Bumpa was the music leader, at Van Dyke Methodist Church in Detroit, under pastor, Dr. Hescott. His son, Don, lives at Gull Lake Bible Conference at this time. Mom went on to be the organist at every church we attended when we were young. I have also given the family other favorites of mine.

"It is my hope that those who attend this celebration leave singing, with joy in their hearts that eternity with God far surpasses any time, accomplishment or happiness here on earth.

"I prefer my remains to not be present at this celebration. I'm not there. Flowers begin to die the moment they are cut for funeral bouquets. Instead, gifts to forward the gospel of Jesus Christ, at Oakland Drive Christian Church, Gull Lake Bible Conference, Promise Keepers, or Day of Discovery, will spread life, and that, everlasting.

"If I should go first and you be left behind..."

"Annabelle, my Annie, my wife, my friend, my companion, my lover, you are so precious, a dear child of God. You love Jesus deeply. You always prayed for me fervently. While very young, you asked God for, and received, a servant's heart toward others. You have used your gift faithfully. I have never been, or felt so loved as from your endless love for me. I love you, dear Annie."

Anne has an astounding understanding of how loving and powerful Jesus is to every part of our life together, as well as that of our children, their spouses, their children, those we have "adopted", and our friends. It is my desire that they would ask God for the same gift He gave her.

"She loves children and is an effective Bible teacher and Christian Storyteller. I had the privilege of teaching the Bible and Bible lessons to adults. Anne helped me learn to share Jesus with children, for which I am forever grateful. Annie has an abundance of love to give. She rescued my love and nurtured me back to an open love to her and others. I would like her to remarry as soon as God sends a man who will love her dearly and care for her tenderly.

"It is my heart's desire that our children, Julie, Susan, and David, their spouses and our grandchildren (and someday great grandchildren), each of whom we love so dearly, declare Jesus as their own personal Savior and live their lives sharing with others His love and power as our Redeemer. (Jas. 1:16) It has been such a blessing to see each of them develop their uniqueness and recognize that God created them that way.

"I have one older brother, Max, and two younger sisters, Marilyn and Janet, who, as children, went out of their way to make my life as normal as possible, loving me and not resenting the extra care it took for me to survive and grow up feeling "normal". They, and most, if not all, of their spouses and children, have made personal commitments to Jesus Christ. Together Anne and I have wonderful nieces and nephews. They are gifted people, who use their gifts for Jesus.

"God designed my life and in the process blessed me with so many wonderful people I've been privileged to know, through church, at Goodwill or the few other places I worked, and throughout the communities where I've lived. Though each person is responsible for the decisions they make, I so wish I had personally shared with each that the start of eternal life with God begins with a personal decision to accept the offer to totally trust Jesus, God's only Son, to be cleansed, thereby removing all sin from our lives, permitting us to enter God's presence. The consequences of that decision are eternal.

"One day, maybe sooner than we want to think, we will all stand before God, the Creator of this universe, to give account for our lives here on earth. If anyone's name is not found written in the Book of Life, he or she will be thrown into the lake of fire. Please. It is my heart's desire to spend "forever"—in heaven—with you.

"As with all people, after someone dies, we should move on with our lives, meeting our needs and letting time mend any hurts. I would encourage you to love each other, especially those we might think are less lovable. May God richly bless each one of you. Give your wife (or husband) a hug every day and tell her/him you love her/him."

JULIE REMEMBERS

The following is Julie's poem that Kathy Young, our pastor's wife, read at Dave's service.

Julie and Stacy meet Dave in Canada at train station

DADDY McWHEELS

Many meet to say farewell
To grieve and share fond tales.
There will be songs of praise
That soothe the heart that ails.

Friends, loved ones, co-workers
Will give comfort to each other.
You'll be missed by one and all
By wife, daughters, son, sisters, brother.

Daddy McWheels, a name we chose
Best describes you to some.
You comforted many and listened to all
Showing others what they could become

You faced adversity many times
Others were unable to survive
Among things like an iron lung
Yet still you were alive.

You helped to make new laws that
Would educate the masses.
As Mr. Goodwill, lives were changed
Through OJT and classes.

While I know you're in a better place
And having a good time too

I wanted to write this poem to say
That I'm going to miss you.

I love you Daddy McWheels.
Your daughter Julie

JESSICA REMEMBERS

In September of 2005, our youngest granddaughter, Jessica, wrote the following school paper when she was ten:

"Grandpa Davey"

"I remember sitting on my grandpa's bed, telling stories when he was young. My grandpa had polio when he was 12 years old. It was very sad when that happened. When my grandpa grew up, he became a boss of a company. He was a very good and nice boss. When he got older he retired. We came over for many sleepovers. We would have a special dinner when we came over and we would play games like tri-ominoes and other games. We would have tons of fun.

At night we would have tea and play Parcheesi.

Then we would get ready for bed and watch a movie. When the movie was done, we would get into our sleeping bags and a pig would guard us, and Grandpa would tell stories when he was little—some stories funny and normal. But they were all good. My grandpa loved pigs. He had pigs all over his room and he had a big stuffed pig. We call him a guard pig.

"This summer, 2005, my grandpa died of old age and polio. He died peacefully. He and grandma were snuggled up together and in the morning my grandpa was dead.

"I had prayed for many years that my grandpa would be able to walk again—and my prayer came true.

By: Jessica Gibson"

OUR SON DAVID REMEMBERS

"How did knowing and living with David Davey affect me?

"David Davey was my father. While I was not born his son, he was my father through the luck of my mother and him getting married. I was lucky enough to have both my biological father and him to be able to call my dad.

"Due to other circumstances, my biological father was out of town, and during the time in my life as I came of age, I was able to live with Dad. As a man grows to adulthood, he needs to see how a man should act to help guide him as he forms his relationships with others around him. I could not have asked for a better man than David to help guide me during those years.

"He possessed all the attributes that help a person to be successful in life. He was caring. He cared for my mother very much. His love for her was deep, and he let this be known. While not overtly demonstrative, his caring glances and soft touches of her let an observer know that they were deeply in love with one another.

"As a young man, if I asked, he would share his wisdom on how to ensure that your relationship with your spouse was so vitally important...to be a team, and the special relationship that God placed in the guardianship of marriage. This relationship is one that is so important in a Christian life, and one that is modeled off Christ's relationship with the church. This, even more to a child, is one that is vitally important to understand.

"He was caring for others. He would help others in many different ways. He would give of his time to some, and of his blessings to others. While I did not see him on a routine basis at work, I knew from the comments that I heard that he helped many. He would offer a helping hand to those who needed it, and a gentle or not so gentle push to those who needed that too. Often times, some people feel that all that is ever needed to help is to give to others, but this is not always the case. Due to upbringing or life circumstances, some people may have developed an attitude of entitlement. Dad was very astute from his experience in Goodwill in being able to see the difference, and when needed, to ensure that personnel were able to grow, and change, and see the value of an honest day's work. At work I know this ensured that many programs were implemented to assist those in his organization to cherish their contribution. Out of his work, if it was a person needing a helping hand, he knew by instinct how to help this person in the way that he/she would be able to best use the assistance.

"He was caring for me. Dad always made time to listen to me. If I was going through the growing pains of a young adult, he was there to talk to me, and help with his wisdom. He never hesitated to take my calls at work, letting me know that I was important. Later, as an adult, I knew that he would drop everything if he needed to, to listen to me and help with guidance. I used him as a mentor, to sound business and personal decisions off. In business, I could count on his experience to think of the different aspects of job opportunities, and how that would affect me as an individual, since he knew me so well. In personal matters, I knew that he would have insight into the right way, and the Christian way of making choices, as well as his knowledge of me as an individual.

"He also taught me honor. He honored God. This helped show those around him how to also honor Him, as well as how to have honor in all aspects of one's life. His love for my mother and how he honored her also helped guide me as a young man in the development of the way that I should honor and respect women. While so many in society devalue respect for others, as well as the respect of women, his example was one that any person, believer or not, could look at and follow his example.

"He shared so many things with me, and helped guide me as I grew. When I think of him, the values that he taught me, besides caring and honor, leap out—integrity, family, sacrifice, courage and commitment, to name the strongest. He was an outstanding man of values, a man that lived what he taught, and a father that I could always look up to. He helped me in so many ways, all through the time that I had the privilege to call him my dad.

"I miss his mentorship now, and while I know he is in a better place, I think of him often. I look forward to the future when I will see him again and let him know how much he helped me to be a better man, a better husband, a better father and Christian, and how much I appreciate that."

DAVE'S LOVE CONTINUES

Dave always kept a clipboard with a lined tablet on it next to his side of our bed. It was nearly a year after he died before I noticed there were several papers under the tablet. When I removed the tablet, I was pleased to see there were many hand written pages. Upon examining them, I discovered two hand-written letters to me that he had written on our twenty-seventh anniversary, only nine months before he died. Each letter was so precious. For some reason, he never gave them to me. He had given me a wonderful hand-made card for that anniversary. These letters are more precious because they were hand written. The two letters read:

LETTER #1

10/29/04

"Dearest Annie,

"How would we have guessed how many wonderful days of love—deep love—God would give to us?

"We know we don't deserve any, but we are so thankful for God's love, care, forgiveness in the precious hours and days He alone has given to us.

"Dearest Annie, these twenty-seven years have been so full and gone by so quickly. Isn't it amazing?

"I am filled with joy as well as happiness over your love for me and my love for you.

"Not only are you faithful, but also giving—far beyond anyone's expectations. You go out of your way to meet my needs, give special and unique care beyond what I think anyone else would ever consider. You do it all with a smile and comfort that is also amazing. Thank you very much.

"I look forward to as many days and years ahead as God will give us. We will use each to strengthen each other, love each other and show His great love to others.

"I love you, forever, without end.

Your David"

LETTER #2

10-29-04

"Dearest Anne,

"Happy Anniversary!

"This one seems more precious than the others. I'm not sure why.

"Who would have thought we would have a 27-year honeymoon and every additional day makes it that much longer. What joy!

"My insides quicken at the sight of you—especially when our eyes meet. That blue. That sparkle.

"My mind drifts to holding your hand at church, in the car, in bed, sitting beside you.

"When I'm cold at night, you know and lean against me, giving warmth. Even when you have to roll away, your foot reaches out to touch mine.

"I have always loved our "night talks." Even though we may be tired, if we awaken at the same time, we need to talk. Sometimes it's about the past day, sometimes about our plans for that day. At times it's about our history—when we were young. You are an Indiana girl, which gives you great authority and credence.

"Even when we are apart, we have a special sense about each other. How many times have you gone shopping only to bring home something I wanted, but had not asked for? I remember you going out of your way home to get a Chicken Coop fish dinner for me, even though you cannot eat fish. That's one recent example among many, many times.

"What has influenced me most is your deep abiding love for God and His Son Jesus. He has been close to you most of your life. He leads your life and relationship with others.

"He has given you a special gift of knowing the real concern of someone who is troubled. You see past the surface to share His love with someone who is hurting.

"I delight in your gift of teaching, especially children. They understand you and what you are sharing with them; you make Scripture clear to them—and, in fact, everyone you witness to.

"You weep for joy at the new believer, cry for sorrow for those that will not give their heart to Jesus, and pray to God like you're having a talk face-to-face. You pray with your heart.

"It's been fun to buy Bibles which are sent to other countries, especially Asian. We've bought many Bible for others—sometimes not knowing who God wanted to receive it. He has been kind enough to usually show us who He wanted to get His Word. I could add more examples.

"It has strengthened my faith—as it has others—to see God work through your life.

"Dearest Annie, we have traveled to places neither of us thought would be possible for us. The fun was doing those things with you.

"Thank you for supporting me, for standing beside me, for giving me strength and having confidence in me. Thank you for wanting to do all this for me, but mostly for your faithful, unwavering, passionate love.

"When we meet in glory, I hope we can remember how wonderfully God let us love each other the few years we had on earth. It has been twenty-seven so far, and I'm ready and eager for more.

Forever,
David"

ANOTHER MESSAGE

The last message Dave typed to anyone in the family was still on his laptop when he died. He wrote it in May when I was in California attending a wedding. Susan and her family were staying here for the two days I was gone. When I read it for the first time, long after his death, I knew that Dave was aware that his days were numbered. I don't think the letter was completed. I know now that, because I loved Dave more than life itself, I never wanted to think of him going, and God leaving me behind, so I never talked to him about his dying. Dave's short message read:

"As I write this, I can tell that my muscles are getting weaker. I sometimes wonder how much longer I will be living this wonderful life with my Annie, before I join our Savior Jesus Christ. Annie, it's been such a great life. If I go first, always remember that no woman has been a better wife than you have been. I feel so loved every day. I appreciate you when you give me aloe lotion back rubs, and massage my entire body. I am grateful for your patience, and for your appreciation for the few things I do for you. You're such a grateful Christian woman. I love our 'night talks' and waking up with your leg across me, or sometimes with your head resting on my stomach. When you're sound asleep that way, and you're hugging my leg or abdomen gently with your hand, I can't help but shed tears of joy and "

FINAL WORDS

This kind and caring, unselfish man was such a blessing to others and me. He always considered other people's needs and never complained. He never talked against anyone and always listened to whatever we had to say. No one was more blessed than our three children, our five grandchildren, and me. He was a five foot, eight-inch gentle giant for God. I know when he walked into Heaven, Dave was greeted with, "Well done, good and faithful servant."

CPSIA information can be obtained
at www.ICGtesting.com
Printed in the USA
FSHW021511210121
77747FS